Rice Bonanza

50 novel rice dishes
from Kashmir to Kerala

Manjira Majumdar

UNICORN BOOKS

Publishers
UNICORN BOOKS Pvt. Ltd., New Delhi-110002
E-mail: unicornbooks@vsnl.com
Website: www.unicornbooks.in • www.kidscorner.in

Distributors
Pustak Mahal, Delhi
J-3/16 , Daryaganj, New Delhi-110002
☎ 23276539, 23272783, 23272784 • *Fax:* 011-23260518
E-mail: info@pustakmahal.com • *Website:* www.pustakmahal.com

Sales Centres
10-B, Netaji Subhash Marg, Daryaganj, New Delhi-110002
☎ 23268292, 23268293, 23279900 • *Fax:* 011-23280567
E-mail: rapidexdelhi@indiatimes.com

Branch Offices
Bangalore: ☎ 22234025
E-mail: pmblr@sancharnet.in • pustak@sancharnet.in
Mumbai: ☎ 22010941
E-mail: rapidex@bom5.vsnl.net.in
Patna: ☎ 3094193 • *Telefax:* 0612-2302719
E-mail: rapidexptn@rediffmail.com
Hyderabad: *Telefax:* 040-24737290
E-mail: pustakmahalhyd@yahoo.co.in

ISBN 81-780-6105-8

Edition : 2006

Printed at : Param Offsetters, Okhla, New Delhi-110020

Dedication

This book is dedicated
to my Parents in Law
Mihir and Ratna Sarkar
and to my Parents
Pronab and Archana Majumdar

Contents

Introduction

The Story of Rice

RICE. Just four letters. Yet, what they conjure up could well be a magician's repertoire of tricks. It forms the base of a culinary adventure, that can take you right across India. Rice is something which, perhaps, unites us all. It is an eating experience that binds us as people of a single nation.

The possibilities that recipes in rice promise are endless. Boiled or steamed, rice can be eaten with a side dish, but prepared with a number of add-ons like vegetables, meats, fish, seafood, mushrooms, dried or fresh fruits and herbs, it is like an orchestra to the palate in which each ingredient is like a separate note but presented together to strike up a symphony of colours, textures and most significantly of taste.

Delicious, yet simple to prepare. This remains the basis of our culinary adventure. You may speak in any of its equivalents, *such as bhaat, chawal, anna, saadam, chokha,* etc. and people in this country, depending on whichever part they come from, will at once, connect. The importance of rice lies in it being the staple food not only across India, but in many other Asian countries, such as China, Japan, Sri Lanka, Thailand, Cambodia and Indonesia, as well. However, the moment you cook rice alongwith something else — it turns into a truly exotic dish.

Simply eaten with a little salt and chillie, as in the rural side or with just a steaming *dal,* topped with a dollop of *ghee*, rice is good enough dish for a whole lot of people daily. Served with the ruby red kidney beans, we in this country, call *rajma*, rice is also good enough to offer to guests. But the moment you say *biryani, pulao* or *fried rice,* rice is turned into something magical.

A sweet rice *pulao* - called *zarda;* lemon rice; *biryani,* rice cooked with meat; *jeera* - cumin rice; *tehri*-rice cooked with a range of vegetables; and even rice pudding like *payesh or payasam,* are some of the special ways in which rice can be prepared and served, particularly in India.

There is enough scope for innovation within the genre of rice, and the quick imaginative housewife can do so much with so little. Apart from the pearly white colour of rice, which when combined with the red, green and yellow of the vegetables presents a virtual feast for the eye, we can also separately prepare yellow, brown and green rice, brought about by the addition of different spices and herbs.

For this is where the homemaker can serve something not only exotic to her guests, but also draw on her imagination to creatively display her culinary talents. She can whip up a most pedestrian dish from its everydayness, into something extra-ordinary.

Rice gives energy and is the best form of carbohydrate. Combined with a variety of other sources – proteins, minerals and vitamins, rice is a wholesome and a nutritiously complete dish in itself. You need not always need a side dish to serve with rice. Pickles, salads and *raita* are just fine as accompaniments if you prepare rice with many things tossed into it.

The quality of rice can vary. It can be long grained or short and broken too. Its consistency in a dish may be fluffy or sticky. Whichever way, there are certain similarities with the Indian rice dishes and with those prepared in many foreign countries too! We all know of the Italian *Risotto, Arborio rice* (a round grained rice grown in northern Italy) cooked in stock with meats and seafood or the *Paella* in Spain or the *Chinese fried rice.* There are so many others that we do not know of.

The Chinese, at home, do eat a rice broth peppered with meats and vegetables (drawing on the vegetables available in their country) but the *Mixed fried rice* is a culinary innovation. It is a culinary invention to make the Chinese cuisine more acceptable and attractive to the non-Chinese, especially those eating at restaurants. Our southern neighbours, the Sri Lankans, have their own version of a *Mulligatawny soup*, thickened with *dal* and garnished with rice, chicken or mutton and vegetables.

Rice can be prepared in a number of ways. Toss in any amount of things into a rice base and see how it gets transformed. Vegetables, seafood, herbs, meats, fowl, fish, tofu, curd, coconut, tamarind nuts, lentils, raisins, dates and even fresh fruits. A rice dish may contain some of the aforesaid items to bring about the sour, tangy, spicy or the sweet taste separately or together in an explosion of flavours.

Even broken wheat, legumes alongwith meat or vegetable stocks can be mixed with rice. Cooked with one or more *dal*, or even with *keema* or mince meat or prawn, rice is turned into *khichdi*, which boasts of its own variety.

Vegetarian *khichdi*, as also rice pudding, is usually offered as *bhog* or a *prasad* offering to the gods and, believe me, as prepared in some temples, it is so divine in taste, that it is indeed fit for the gods!

Eating rice, perhaps, keeps the country together. It is a regular feature in any urban dining table, though ready-to-cook meals are a common feature these days. This includes the specially cooked rice too. Even if the North is considered more of a wheat eating zone and the South Indians are generally taken as the veritable rice eaters, its popularity criss crosses the entire country.

The scent of the long *Basmati rice* mingling with saffron or the parboiled rice spiked with humble mustard seeds, can be as divergent as sumptuous. Unlike what is commonly perceived, a rice dish can be created in a jiffy and can be made so appetizing to wean your hungry children away from fast food, synonymous with junk food.

The universal appeal of rice is growing fast. Rice eating is not just restricted to India. The West, too, is increasingly waking up to the goodness of rice. With the best kind of rice grains being exported there from Asia, its popularity in the western countries is fast soaring. Unfortunately, we in India, overlook its true value, sometimes.

Rice eating has been prevalent in India from the ancient times as old texts mention its presence in some form or the other. Indian history has it that rice was cultivated from the times of the Indus Valley Civilization. It was found as a wild plant but slowly, it evolved over the years to its present state.

Rice, as research tells us, was cooked among the Arabs, as stuffings into the stomachs of chickens, which was then stuffed into goats, and finally stuffed into camels! This rice, mixed with dates and other dried fruits, was slow cooked for hours. So you can imagine the variety of flavours mingling with it! Another dish, *Hamin*, mixes meat, legumes and short-grained rice together to cook over a slow fire before being served by the Jews during *Sabbath*. One wonders whether *Halim*, which is eaten by the Muslim, draws its inspiration from it. The latter may not contain rice but is quite basic, what with wheat *dalia,* various kinds of lentil or *dal* and of course, meats, cooked over a slow fire for an entire day. It can be eaten anytime of the day, garnished with herbs, to provide both taste and nutrition.

The Spanish may have learnt to eat rice from their invaders, the Moors, who influenced the architectural styles and cuisine in the Iberian peninsula. *Paella,* a rice *pilaf,* or *pilau* (rice cooked with meat and vegetables originated from Turkey) consists of rice mixed with all kinds of meats and shrimps and in it, is used saffron, whose weight is almost measured in gold, adding that golden yellow tint to the rice.

Remember the famous feisty New Orleans song, *Jambalaya crayfish pier fillet gumbo* from the lap of Louisiana state? Known as Cajun *country,* (descendents of French Canadians settled here) both Cajuns and Creoles (who are a racial mix of coloured Caribbeans with Europeans) were concentrated in this southern state of the United States. They prepare both *gumbo* - a kind of okra *(bhindi)* with rice, fish and chicken base and *jambalaya,* which is a very popular dish prepared with rice, chicken and shrimps. It's a very old dish that combines seafood, meat, vegetables, green pepper, cayenne pepper, celery and onions. With an addition of tomatoes, the colour turns reddish, while without tomatoes, it remains just brown. In Africa, among the Nigerians, a rice dish called *Jollof* is made with rice, tomato paste, red pepper, meat, fish, vegetables and various spices.

Where does one start mapping the rice route in India? Where does the journey start and where does it end ? For instance, the Britishers in India, woke up to a morning breakfast of *Kedigree* (forerunner to the *khichdi* maybe), literally a mish mash of a mound of rice, green chillies, butter, eggs, dried fish, salt; all mixed up and eaten very hot.

This book attempts to take you through the kitchens of India, to bring you the various simple rice dishes cooked within innumerable types of homes. I have tried to be as exhaustive as possible to include as many regions as possible, but it is a subjective book; of eaten and tried recipes and there may be other rice dishes too that I may have overlooked. However, I keep my eyes, ears and mostly, my taste buds open.

There are some regions which may be conspicuous by their absence. Like the seven states of the North-East, which merits separate attention. I have left out both Rajasthan and Madhya Pradesh, though the *Bhopali pulao* is quite famous for its add-ons in rice, mainly of diced carrots and shelled peas.

Apart from this, I think I have been fairly exhaustive, including certain innovative dishes that are a result of urbanization and blending of various culinary schools. Sometimes, one tries to replicate what is eaten in a restaurant, by bringing together certain tastes or fusing some ingredients to create a new taste. Some of the recipes included in the book have grown out of that too.

Many women, young and old, working or simply homemakers, friends and relatives have shared their culinary secrets. The emphasis is on dishes that take between 15 to 30 minutes to get together and about the same time-range to cook.

I have not gone into the details of the various types of rice grown in India and abroad. It is said that there are more than a lakh varieties of rice in India alone! Rice is connected with so many rituals and festivals, where special rice dishes are eaten. Not just this, rice has also spawned poems, songs and literature.

In traditional Hindu weddings, rice plays a significant role. In the western parts of the country, the young bride who enters her in-laws' home, tips over a pot of rice with her feet. The rice grains, filled to the brim, scatters. This signifies the advent of Goddess Lakshmi, bringing wealth and prosperity into the house, measured in grains of rice!

The Indian rice is known as the *rice indica* and is eaten with hands. This is the smooth white or creamy grain that gets fluffy after cooking. In Japan, rice is evolved as *japonica,* a more sticky variety, which is more convenient to eat with chopsticks. Many people of South Eastern Asia also eat rice noodles made from the *javanica* variety.

Every region in India concentrates on a particular type of rice for taste and texture and it is all about how it is processed after being grown—Smooth and long grained or roughly textured and broken.

This book is all about nutritiously, both pressure and pan cooked rice (we are not talking about the *dum pukht* style, though you may try that, once in a while) aimed for today's busy women or even a man You cook with what is readily available in the markets/ supermarkets, and there is a whole lot of options for the buyers and consumers here.

From various home kitchens which I have raided and reasonably the superb cooks, whose brains I have picked, here are about 50 rice dishes with their regional highlights. These include both vegetarian and non-vegetarian, rice desserts and just one snack. That is, something that can be made with left-over rice!

I have consciously left out dishes where rice is grounded and used as an ingredient as in food like *dosas, idlis* or Indian cookies. The basic taste of rice has not been tampered with.

Enjoy rice, the best way you can. The rice dishes form a vibrant example of the Indian cuisine kaleidoscope, which has received and absorbed so many influences, brought about waves of invasion and immigration and finally, assimilation of so many cultures and civilizations. It has evolved into something essentially rich and extremely palatable.

Some Common Tips

Some of the steps in cooking rice are common in most cases. Hence, to avoid monotony, we give the hints once and for all.

Rice has first to be picked clean. With fine Basmati grain, coming packaged, this can be given a miss, but most raw rice has to be first cleaned of dirt particles (sometimes, even small stones) and then washed well. Change the water in which you are washing the rice, at least thrice. Drain off the water well. In case of fried rice, this must be even more so.

Rice kept soaked in water for sometime, cooks faster and does not increase in volume, but this is not mandatory. It can however, soak while you get the other ingredients together; chopping vegetables, for instance. The water level in the soak should not be over an inch, unless specified otherwise.

A pinch of *haldi* or turmeric powder *mixed in a little milk,* added to the rice, gives it a nice yellow colour. In fact, it can work as a substitute for the more expensive saffron (also to be mixed with a bit of milk). Saffron, of course, gives a unique flavour to the dish besides that subtle yellow-orange colour. A regal touch!

It has been our endeavour to give all measurements as accurately as possible. But often, a cook's discretion is a must. For four, generally would mean 4 adults or maybe 2 adults and three children.

Regarding the servings, one kg. of rice cooked with either vegetables or meat, would definitely feed about six to eight people, but again, it would depend on whether you are serving only a rice dish or not. One to two cups, (depending on the size of the cups) would easily feed a family of four adults.

Obviously, rice will cook faster in a pressure cooker than in an open pan. Both chicken and fish cook faster than mutton, so combining these with rice will not take too much time, but make sure of using very tender pieces, when mutton is used.

We all know that pressure cooking is quick, therefore, all the ingredients can be mixed and cooked at one go. In cases where the rice and the other ingredients have been cooked three-fourths and separately, blending and cooking these together should be done in an open pan, just before serving.

Please note: If rice has been cooked separately before blending it with the other ingredients, make sure, the water in the rice has been well drained of. Gently and evenly mix together both the rice and the add-ons. Rice cooks just right both in a pressure cooker or in a rice cooker, after the water has been adjusted – in most cases, one inch above the rice level. For two *katori(s)* or small bowls of rice, you will roughly need three *katori(s)* of water. *More water may be necessary when cooking in an open pan, where the water can be adjusted from time to time.*

In case you are cooking in a pressure cooker, turn the flame off after the first whistle. Exceptions have been noted.

By an open pan, we also mean a *handi* or a *degchi.* There are so many smart cook-and-serve utensils available in the market today. Some of these make it possible to cook with very little oil.

Usually, in a mixed rice dish, the vegetables or meats are prepared in a separate vessel, for which a *kadai* or *wok* is fine.

It is advisable to microwave after adjusting the time (which varies from oven to oven) and only after keeping the rice sealed in with the juices from the meat or vegetables. Grease with adequate water or otherwise, as in the case of baking. If not done so, there is a chance of the rice turning hard and very grainy.

Please remember that if the stock in which the meat or vegetable has been boiled, is used as a substitute for water in which to cook the rice, the dish will taste much better. A stock can also be prepared by boiling chicken soup cubes available in the market.

If vegetables in *pulao/fried rice* are to retain their crispness, stir fry these separately and keep aside. Only cook these with the rice for a few minutes before serving or they turn limp.

As an option, for the long grained *pulao*, you may add just a pinch of sugar to the raw rice for this helps to keep the grains separate from each other. In some other cases, a pinch of sugar is added while cooking, for taste.

If the rice is boiled separately before the other ingredients are added, a little bit of salt can be added. The final seasoning can all be added later.

By flame, we mean the gas flame. Slow cooking, is putting it on *dum, almost akin to baking*. The modern and convenient way would be, when the pot containing the rice dish is placed on a *tawa* or griddle on low heat, the lid of the pot has to be secured tight so that no steam escapes. Since this takes time, the trick is to cook a dish almost three-fourths and then put it on *dum*, for that finishing touch! If cooking in a pressure cooker, do not open the lid immediately on turning the flame off. Only open the clutch of the pressure cooker handle and let the latter open on its own after the steam gradually escapes. This will help keep all the aroma sealed.

The sweet dishes made with rice and milk should be stirred in a heavy bottomed pan so that the milk and the rice do not burn.

Quality of rice: The quality of rice depends on how it is processed. The fine grained Basmati rice works best for *biryani* and *pulao,* but ordinary polished or the *atop (Gobind Bhog)* variety can do also when we refer to a quick home dish with whatever is available at hand. Parboiled rice is acceptable in certain cases. For an everyday *khichdi,* all types of rice can be used because it turns into a gruel-like consistency. But cooked with good rice, it will give a great taste. In Assam, however, *Bora Chawal* is used for both savoury and sweet rice. It is dark reddish in colour and is the newly harvested rice. So, it is a little sticky in nature.

Now let us give few thoughts on the *raita* or the salad made with curd/yoghurt. You may serve these rice dishes with a gravy or curry of your choice, but a wholesome *raita* is adequate and complements the dish. In a *raita,* you can add vegetables like potatoes, *bhindi,* carrots, brinjals, etc. If the rice dish is very hot and spicy, you can serve a *raita* made with a fruit like pineapple, too! In case of a not-so-hot rice preparation, you can spice up the *raita* with onions, chillies and herbs.

Finally, we leave the cooking medium flexible. While white oil, *ghee* and butter are mentioned, what you use and how much of it should be used is your choice entirely. You can fry in as much as a couple of teaspoons of oil or in one big tablespoon. In some cases, oil and *ghee* are combined in a fifty-fifty ratio, so you have the benefit of both. One for health and the other for taste. Overall, the accent is on healthy cooking.

Some measurements are given in grams and some in teaspoons/tablespoons (tsp/tbsp).

Some Common Names

Indian spices and certain cooking terms, by now, are well known and are available all over the world. Here are some of their common names for reference.

Common Language – English

Aaloo — Potatoes

Aaloo-Bhukhara/Alucha — Plums

Aam/Amra — Mango

Adrak — Ginger

Ajwain — Carom seeds

Akhrot — Walnuts

Amrud — Guava

Anaar — Pomegranate

Annanas — Pineapple

Angoor — Grapes

Amchur — Mango powder

Amla — Gooseberry

Arbi — Colocosia

Arhar — Toor dal

Baingan — Brinjal/Egg Plant

Badam — Almonds

Badi Ilaichi — Black cardamoms

Baking Powder — Baking Powder

Besan — Bengal gram powder

Bhakri — Crisp roti

Bhat — Rice preparation

Bhindi — Lady Fingers/Okra

Bhutta — Corn

Boondi — Deep-fried droplets of pulse flour

Chai — Tea

Chapati — Flat griddle-roasted wheat circlet

Chat — Combination of food items, chutneys and spices

Chat Masala — Powdered spices used for chat

Chenna — Cottage cheese *(paneer)*

Chironji — Chiroli

Cholia — Green gram

Chote Aaloo — Baby potatoes

Chote Tamatar — Cherry tomatoes

Choti Ilaichi — Green cardamoms

Chukander — Beetroot

Chutney — Spicy sauce of various combinations of food items grounded together

Common Language – English

Dahi — Curd

Dalchini — Cinnamon sticks

Dalia — Broken wheat used for porridge

Desi Ghee — Clarified butter

Dhania — Coriander seeds

Doodh — Milk

Falooda — A drink made of corn flour noodles added to sweetened and flavoured milk

France Beans — French beans

Gajar — Carrot

Ghee — Vanaspati ghee

Ghenhu — Wheat

Gobi — Cauliflower

Gosht — Mutton/Meat

Gur/Guda — Coarse brown sugar

Haldi — Turmeric

Halwa — Semi solid sweet confection

Hara Badam — Fresh green almonds

Hara Channa — Green gram

Hara Dhania — Coriander leaves

Hara Pyaj — Spring onions

Hari Mirchi — Green chili

Hari Gobi — Broccoli

Hari Chutny — Ground paste of fresh coriander and mint leaves with green chili and ginger, etc

Heeng — Asafoetida

Imli — Tamarind

Imli Chutney — Spicy sauce made of tamarind pulp

Jaiphal — Nutmeg

Javiatri — Mace

Jeera — Cumin seeds

Jilebi/Jalebi — Coiled tubular fried pastry soaked in sugar syrup

Kabab — Spit roasted pieces of vegetables, meats or paneer

Kabuli Channa — Chic peas

Kachori — Stuffed flour patty

Kadi Patta — Curry leaves

Kaju — Cashew nuts

Kala Namak — Rock salt

Kala Channa — Bengal gram

Kali Mirch (Kali Miri) — Black pepper

Karela — Bitter gourd

Kas — Grated

Kela — Banana

Kesar — Saffron

Khajur — Dates

Khaskhas — Poppy seeds

Kheema — Minced meat

Kheer — Milk and rice sweet dish

Khichdi — Rice and pulse dish

Kishmish — Raisins

Khoya/Mawa — Dry condensed milk used for making Indian sweets

Khumb — Mushrooms

Khumani/khurmani — Apricots

Common Language – English

Kofta — Grated vegetables or minced meat, seasoned and mixed with a winding, steamed or deep fried and served with any gravy.

Kulfi — A frozen confection, made of thickened milk and set in metal cones.

Lal Mirch — Red Chilie

Lassi — Butter milk / A drink made of curds

Lavang — Cloves

Lehsun — Garlic

Litchi — Litchi fruit

Machhi — Fish

Madhu/Shahad — Honey

Makhan — Butter

Makki — Maize

Malai — Fresh cream

Maida — Refined flour

Mattar — Green peas

Maash/Urad — Black gram

Masoor Dal — Lentils

Methi — Fenugreek

Methre — Fenugreek seeds

Safed Mirch — White Pepper

Moong — Moong dal

Moong Dhuli — Moong (Split)

Muli — Raddish

Mungphali — Peanuts/Groundnuts

Munakka — Sultanas

Murgi or Murg — Chicken

Namak — Salt

Naan — Leavened bread baked in tandoor

Nariyal — Coconut

Nashpati — Pears

Nimbu — Lemon

Palak — Spinach

Paneer — Cottage cheese

Paneer ka Pani — Whey

Papad — Crisp sun-dried waffers

Papita — Papaya

Payesh — A milk-rice dish

Phal — Fruits

Phulka/Roti — Dry puffed wheat circlet

Pilav/Pulao — Meat or vegetables rice dish

Pista — Pistachio nuts

Pratha — Layered roti fried on griddle or roasted in tandoor

Pua — Sweet confection

Pudina — Mint leaves

Puri — Crisp deep fried wheat snack

Pyaj — Onions

Rabbri — Clotted cream flakes

Raie — Mustard seeds

Rajma — kidney beans

Rasa — An extract/juice

Rava — Semolina

Safed Makhan — White home-made butter

Common Language – English

Sag — Leafy vegetables or a dish made of them

Sarson — Mustard

Saunf — Fennel/Aniseed

Sev — Apple

Sepreta Doodh — Toned milk

Sherbet — A cool drink made of any fruit juice or Rose flower

Sirka — Vinegar

Suji — Semolina

Sukha Meva — Dry fruits

Soya Paneer — Toffu

Tamatar — Tomato

Tamater Pulp — Tomato puree

Tandoor — An open clay oven

Tandoori — Any food cooked in tandoor

Tarkari — Vegetables

Tatri — Citric acid

Tejpatta — Bay leaf

Tel — Oil or cooking oil

Til — Sesame seeds

Tulsi — Basil

Urad Dal — Black gram

Varan — A dal dish made of Tuvar Dal

Wadian — Fermented and spiced pulse-vegetables lumps. Sun-dried, steamed/cooked with dals and vegetables

Zaffran — Kesar

Zarda — Sweet rice preparation

Conversion Guide

1 tablespoon — 15 ml

1 teaspoon — 5 ml

a pinch — $^1/_8$ teaspoon

¼ cup — 60 ml (4 tablespoons)

$^1/_3$ cup — 80 ml (5½ tablespoons)

½ cup — 125 ml (8 tablespoons)

$^2/_3$ cup — 160 ml (10½ tablespoons)

$^3/_4$ cup — 175 ml (12 tablespoons)

1 cup — 250 ml (16 tablespoons)

1 level measure* of **Sugar Free** powder concentrate = 1 teaspoon of sugar

1 level measure of **Sugar Free** powder concentrate = 1 pellet of Sugar Free

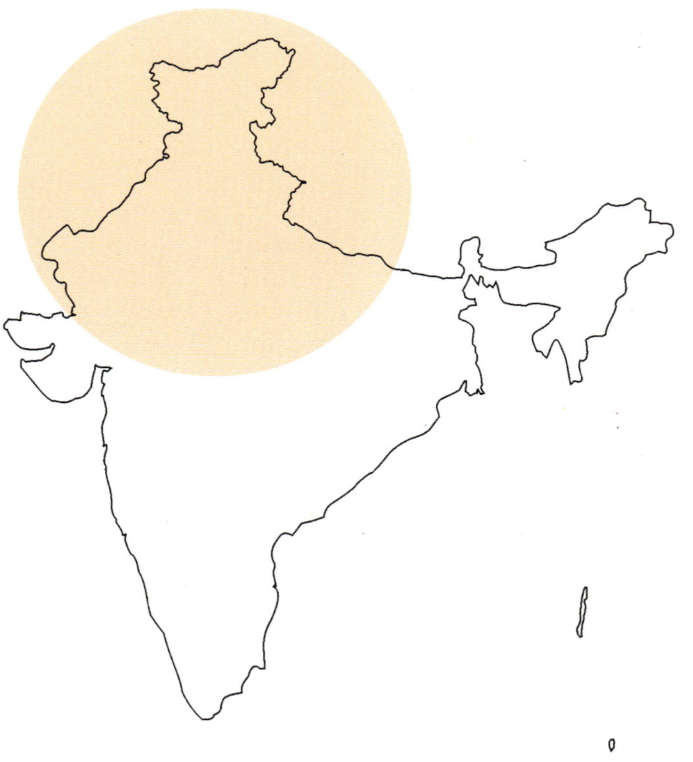

Section 1

Chawal

In the northern parts of India, rice is called as *Chawal*. Following are the preparations with Rice or *Chawal*.

1. **Kashmir :** *Yakhni Pulao* – Popular in Northern India.
2. **Punjab :** *Tehri*
3. **Delhi :** *Jeera rice*
4. **Uttar Pradesh :** *Meat pulao*

The northern part of India, and that would today roughly mean the territories of Kashmir, Punjab, Haryana, Rajasthan, and Western Uttar Pradesh is not exactly known for its rice eaters. There were parts of this region that once belonged to India, but now belongs to Pakistan. These were the western parts of Punjab and the entire region of Sindh stretching up to the Kutch area. However, when these parts were together, they once made up the great **Indus Valley Civilization**.

This ancient civilization, bears the testimony to a crop like millet, consumed in various forms. Some of the ancient Vedas mention this too.

However, signs of a wild variety of a rice plant is also recorded in history; most probably an import from the Far East. The traces of the same plant were also found during the Aryan Civilization in India. However, the Aryan's sacrificial offerings talk more of ghee, milk and honey, than rice.

The North Western frontier stretching from Afghanistan up to almost the Middle East is said to have eaten down the ages, unleavened bread or *chapati* made in clay ovens, known popularly as the *tandoor*. Obviously, these *chapati(s)* were made with wheat and how much of it was grown and whereof, remains outside the purview of this book.

Suffice to say, rice eating came to the northern plains gradually; the result of a slow infusion of a certain give and take. One fact is very clear. Rice is a delicacy in the north. It may not be eaten in great quantities as in the south or in the eastern part, but say *rajma chawal* to any North Indian, and his eyes will light up. Punjabis chuck in the season's vegetables into a vegetarian *pulao*, known as *tehri*, and the Sindhis have their own way of preparing this. In fact, *tehri* is popular throughout Uttar Pradesh, even in the hilly parts which has been carved into a new state known as Uttaranchal.

Among the *Uttar Pradeshis*, those belonging to the eastern part, eat more rice than their western counterparts. The Mathurs, a Kayastha community of Uttar Pradesh, known for their proximity to the ruling Mughals at one time, imbibed non-vegetarian influences into their cuisine. They eat a special meat *pulao*, rather like the *yakhni pulao*, made by the Kashmiris. This is not quite the *biryani*, but delectable nevertheless.

Kashmiris, on the other hand, are great rice eaters. Perhaps, this is more for the calories that rice possesses, the starchy nature emits heat, helping to keep the people warm in colder climates.

1. Kashmir

Snow-capped mountains framing a lush green valley forms the rural backdrop, as *Kashmiris* sit around the fire, relishing hot food and cheerful conversation. Flakes of snow flit by the window as they enjoy their saffron-flavoured tea and often, mouthfuls of rice, eaten with a vegetable preparation and possibly a dried meat dish.

Of course, available too are many forms of Indian breads, made from wheat or flour. On the other hand, there are quite a few rice dishes to be enjoyed in the Valley, of which the mutton *Yakhni Pulao*, is a popular one. Such is the magic of the Valley, that this dish is not a stress on the digestive system; rather, a combination with other ingredients, make it a balanced meal.

Both the Hindus and Muslims of Kashmir are meat eaters. *Kashmiri Hindus*, (Brahmins or Pandits), as they are known, like their counterparts in Bengal, and unlike the Brahmins of Maharashtra and South India, also eat fish. On *Shivaratri*, Lord Shiva is offered a meal of fish and rice in Kashmir.

Apart from the well-known *Rogan Josh*, the red mutton curry, enjoyed equally with rice and *roti*, the Valley is known for a number of other delicacies, as part of the *wazwan* banquet, prepared by professional cooks. The state is noted for many dishes flavoured with saffron, the spice got from the Crocus plant that grows profusely in this state.

My friend, Anju Munshi, a freelance writer and a great homemaker, has done a book on Kashmiri cuisine, that is both healthy and easy to prepare. She shares her recipe for the *Yakhni Pulao* with me.

Anju says, "For a Kashmiri woman, cooking and serving are not arduous or depressing chores. They enjoy doing it. There are times, however, when she feels like resorting to short cuts or is in the mood to serve a one-dish meal."

This is where her *Yakhni Pulao,* comes in handy, as it combines taste with a certain simplicity, though *yakhni* or curd, is not always used in cooking the meat.

In some other cases, *Yakhni Pulao,* is rice cooked in the stock of lamb or chicken that has been delicately flavoured with aromatic spices.

ANJU 's *Yakhni Pulao*

Serves 4-6.

For the mutton balls or *kofta(s).*

Ingredients

• Chicken mince	500 gms
• Onion paste	1 tsp
• Garlic and ginger paste	1 tsp
• *Garam masala* powder	1 tsp
• Curd *(optional)*	A tbsp
• Egg	1 (well beaten white portion)
• Salt	To taste

For the *pulao*.

Ingredients

• Basmati Rice	500 gms
• Asafoetida	A pinch
• Cloves	A few
• Cinnamon	2 sticks
• Green cardamoms	3-4 crushed
• Water	5 cup
• Oil	2 tbsps
• Aniseed	4 tsps

Method

Mix the mince with all the ingredients. Make walnut-sized balls. Lightly fry in a pan and keep aside. Meanwhile, heat oil in another pan, add the rice, washed and dried, alongwith the spices and pastes, meant for the rice. Keep stirring for five minutes. Add the water and cook till done. Take out the rice carefully off the fire and spread it out on a big open dish.

Now mix the fried mince balls to the rice, add coriander leaves and put it back in the pan in which the rice was cooked. Return to the fire and cook for about 15 minutes, till the rice and the meat are well blended.

Garnish with onion rings.

Serve with pickles, chutneys or dips of your choice.

2. Punjab

Punjab is the land of wheat, corn and bright yellow fields of mustard. Its robust sense of life extends into its cuisine like *sarson da saag* (mustard leaves-preparation) and *makki di roti* (*chapati* made of corn).

When I was growing up, in a very cosmopolitan Calcutta presently called as Kolkata, our Punjabi neighbours would tease my *chapati*-preferring younger sister, by saying, "Wait till you grow up, we will marry you off to a *Sardarji!*" With no offence meant to Sikhs, this was one of the scary reasons for me to turn into a rice lover. Both rice and wheat have their own merits but for many, their daily diet is not complete without at least two tablespoons of rice!

Throughout the north, including a state like Uttaranchal, one hears of a one-meal rice dish called *tehri*. This is a no-frill rice dish, it is a mixed vegetable *pulao* prepared fresh with the best of winter vegetables like cauliflower, carrot, beet, peas and tomato, and eaten steaming hot on a winter afternoon. Really, this is an unbeatable 'rice' experience.

I learnt about the *tehri* in Delhi, at the home of the filmmaker and television producer, Ramesh Sharma of *New Delhi Times*, fame. It was prepared by his mother, Raji aunty, who is no more. But she will always be remembered as an extraordinary woman. Generous, affectionate and efficient, she never resented guests, who dropped in without prior appointment. Rather, she used to get busy in the kitchen to feed them.

I remember, she said, "*Tehri* is usually made in Punjab as elsewhere in the north, as a one-dish meal with left over cooked vegetables (you can add whatever vegetable is at hand and there are no rules that it must contain just this and this and no more). You can make it rich by adding spices like *garam masala* or prepare it simply." The best part of it is, in each home, the same *tehri* tastes different.

And talking about vegetable *pulao,* a Sindhi friend said, her aunt prepared one by adding a nice green chutney, made with mint and coriander leaves to it. She failed to give me the recipe, though!

RAJI AUNTY's *Tehri*

Serves 4-6.

Ingredients

• Basmati/Dehra Dun Rice	½ kg
• Sliced vegetables	2 cups of diced (into medium size) carrots, capsicum, cauliflower, potatoes, tomatoes, beet, etc.
• Shelled peas	½ cup
• White oil	2 tbsps
• Sliced onions	2
• Green chillies	A few
• Whole *Garam masala*	4 big *elaichies*, a couple of small *elaichies*, 2 *laung* sticks and one stick of *dalchini*
• *Tej patta* (bay leaves)	A few
• Salt	To taste
• Coriander leaves	To garnish

Method

In a pressure cooker, pour the oil and when smoking, add the *tej patta* and onion slices and fry it till it is light brown. Add the green chillies and slit these slightly when tossing them around. Then, one by one, add the vegetables, taking care to add those that take a while to cook first, for example, potatoes. Lastly, add the capsicum, for over fried and boiled capsicum lose their flavour. Finally, add tomatoes, for these also cook very fast. Add the whole *garam masala* and stir fry these with rice which has been already cleaned and washed.

You may add a pinch of *haldi.* The various colours of the vegetables segue into the dish. Add water accordingly and cook only till the first whistle or everything will turn very soggy. Long grained Basmati rice cooks fast so it will synchronize with the time needed to cook the sliced vegetables, which need not be boiled before. Serve hot.

Please note: This dish is more of an everyday one. You may cook it like the Chinese Mixed Fried rice where the vegetables are stir fried very crisp separately before being added to the dish or as instructed, you may cook it all together!

This rice dish retains just enough moisture released from the tomatoes and other vegetables to make it soft but never gooey. The fresh sweet taste of the winter vegetables blend into it so well that there is no need for any other accompaniments, except maybe a mixed pickle.

3. Delhi

The favoured capital of Muslim India and later of British India and now, India's capital city, with the prefix 'New', contains many a Delhi within it. There were seven Delhi(s) and history informs us that it would be difficult to pinpoint the real character of Delhi, today. So many communities from all over India, have made this city their home, besides pouring in for higher education and employment opportunities. This has resulted in a rich and truly melting pot of cuisine.

When we refer to a certain Mughlai cuisine, we have parts of North India in mind, where the Muslim invasion in waves resulted in fusion cooking of a different sort. Take the case of *biryani*, for instance. It was not exactly a direct import from Turkey, where the *pilaf* or the *pulao,* i.e., rice cooked with meat and vegetables is believed to have originated.

Under Persian and other Central Asian influences, *biryani* as a highly esteemed rice dish, evolved in various ways in different parts of India. The word *biryani* — Persian in origin, means grilled or fried. The meat is thus prepared before it is mixed with rice, seasoned with a magic portion of certain spices that are India's contribution to the culinary world.

The different types of *biryani* eventually, came to be known by different names. For instance, ***Noormahal Biryani*** contains *chicken koftas* flavoured with special spices, whereas in ***Nawabi Hyderabad***, it was prepared differently.

In some ways, Delhi is also synonymous with Uttar Pradesh. As Lucknow and Rampur are famous for so many culinary delights of rice, so too is Delhi. Apart from the meat-based *biryani*, Uttar Pradesh is also rich in *vegetarian pulao*(s). A *sweet pulao*, called *Zarda* (included in the miscellaneous section); a sweet- sour *pulao*, called *Mutanjan*; *Baghera Chawal*, which is cooked with fresh ginger and garlic; *Peas Pulao* and *Jeera Rice* are some of these. The last mentioned is cooked in homes throughout the north on occasions when special rice is served, and is a regular item on menus in restaurants serving Indian cuisine.

Teamed with a vegetarian or a non-vegetarian side dish or eaten with a *boondi raita*, it is a delightful experience of smooth rice, subtly mixed with the crunchy white *jeera*.

MAYA BASU 's *Jeera Rice*

Mrs Maya Basu, a Delhite, is a *Probashi Bangali*, meaning a Bengali, who is settled outside Bengal. She grew up in Delhi and graduated from the Delhi University and retired as manager of a public sector undertaking. Being a working woman, she devised many short cuts in her kitchen to balance her housekeeping and a career. Even now, in her mid-seventies, she loves to invite relatives and friends for a nice home-cooked meal. The best meal, she confesses, she ever had was a simple dish of rice and *dal* at a *dhaba*, (a roadside eatery). "Run by a Punjabi refugee, it was one of the many that were located at the Lajpat Market," she reminisces. Those familiar with Delhi, will at once identify Lajpat Nagar in South Delhi, when in fact, it used to be a refugee market behind the Red Fort.

Refugees, from what is today Pakistan, sold food in makeshift stall here, she recalls, "One such stall owner sold long-grained fragrant Basmati rice, with steaming *Arhar dal,* topped with a spoonful of *desi ghee* for a very nominal amount. There were other food items sold such as hot *gulab jamuns,* for instance, but the taste of the rice and *dal* still lingers in my tongue".

I give below two of Maya Basu's recipes; a result of a certain culinary fusion, no doubt. First, is a simple *Jeera Rice,* she learnt from watching a friend's mother, who had learnt it from her mother-in-law, an old lady, hailing from Uttar Pradesh. Mrs Basu modifies it by using less of the ghee. In fact, to keep it as healthy as possible; instead of cooking it in ghee, she cooks it in white oil. However, prior to cooking, she mixes the rice with a little ghee, so that, the scent of the ghee gets into the dish, without making it too greasy.

The second dish is *Jeera Rice with fish* but with boneless variety of fish. Bengalis will be Bengalis, wherever they may be, especially when it comes to the fishy matter. And who does not know about the fish market of Chittaranjan Park, where nearly half of Delhi's Bengalis live. Mrs Basu now lives a stone's throw from this market, a tad nostalgic about her old home in crowded Daryaganj.

Serves 2-3.

Ingredients

- Fine grained Basmati Rice — 1 big cup full
- Ghee — 1 tbsp
- Whole white *jeera* — ½ to ¾th tsp

• Green chillies	A couple (split and deseeded)
• Grated ginger	$1/4^{th}$ inch
• White oil	2 tbsps
• Salt	To taste

Method

Wash rice well and drain the water. Mix the rice well with ghee, chillies and salt to taste and set aside. Heat oil and when smoking, add the *jeera* and grated ginger.

When brown, add the rice and stir it around for sometime, till the rice and *jeera* are well blended. Add the water and slow cook in an open pan till water is used up and rice is cooked.

Optional: (You may cook it with a quarter cup of shelled green peas.)

There is another version or way to cook this dish. You first make the rice and keep aside. In hot oil, fry one large sliced onion. When nicely browned, add *jeera.* To the spluttering *jeera,* add the cooked rice and mix it around or temper *(tadka)* the rice with the browned onion slices and *jeera.*

Eat hot, either with a gravy dish or a *boondi raita (at room temperature).*

Jeera Rice with Fish

Serves 3-4.

Ingredients

• Boneless fish	400 gm (*Bhetki* or *Rohu*) cubed
• Ingredients for rice	The same as Jeera Rice

Method

Coat fish pieces with a little salt and red chilli powder as per taste. Deep fry in about 2 tbsps of white oil and set aside.

When the *jeera* rice is almost done, add the fish pieces and see to it that there is enough moisture remaining in the rice. Simmer it for 5 to 7 minutes.

Serve with *boondi or onion raita.*

4. Uttar Pradesh

We have seen how the rice is cooked in various ways in the most populated state of India, i.e., UP in the section on Delhi. No discussion on rice would be complete without the mention of the Mathur community of Uttar Pradesh. I would not have had the fortune of knowing this *Kayastha* community of UP, had not my cousin sister, Radhika Ramnath, been a half Mathur. Her mother belonged to the large Bahadur clan of Civil Lines, Old Delhi, once the walled city.

The Bahadur family reflects a certain *olde worlde* gracious living with erudition much like their cuisine. Madhur Jaffrey, actress and television personality, a great foodie herself, belongs to this same clan. Mathurs enjoy their drinks with kebabs, and no festive occasion or marriage celebration is complete without a few non-vegetarian dishes.

Mrs Om Lata Bahadur, Radhika's aunt is a gracious hostess. Her *pulao*, cooked with mutton, comes closest to the *Yakhni pulao* of Kashmir. She shares her way of doing this greatly appreciated *mutton pulao* as described in the following page:

OM LATA BAHADUR's *Meat Pulao*

Serves 10-12.

Ingredients

• Rice	1 kg
• Mutton	2 kg
• Onions	2 (medium size and thinly sliced)
• Tomato	2 (large ones–grated)
• Salt	To taste
• Oil	4 tbsps
• G*aram masala* (whole)	
• *Elaichis*	4 big black
• Green *elaichis*	4 small
• *Tej patta* (bay leaf)	2
• *Laung*	7-8
• *Dalchini* (optional)	7-8
• *Kali mirch* (pepper corns)	8 pieces
• *Garam masala* grounded	2 tsps

Method

Measure the rice with a *katori* so that the water can be adjusted. Wash the rice well and soak it for half an hour.

Put the meat along with a little salt and half of the whole *garam masala* in about 1 litre of water (4 glasses). Boil until half cooked. Take the meat out and put aside. Keep the water also aside separately to be used later for cooking the *pulao*.

Fry half the onions until half-brown and keep aside.

Now put the rest of the onions into a *degchi* or a saucepan alongwith the rest of the whole *garam masala* and sauté it a little. Put in the rice and fry it for about 5 minutes. Add the grated tomatoes and mix them well into the rice. Add the grounded *garam masala* powder and salt, and turn it into the rice so that it mixes well.

Now add the meat pieces. Mix well. Put the water from the boiled meat (that had been kept aside), adding additional fresh water as necessary to make it double the amount of rice. Cook until the meat is tender and the rice is cooked just right. Put a lid on the cooked *pulao*, after taking it off the fire for keeping the flavour intact. Before serving, garnish with the browned onions which have been kept aside.

Please note: You may prepare the meat before and keep it aside. The rice, should, however, be cooked before it is served so that it remains hot with its flavour intact.

East India

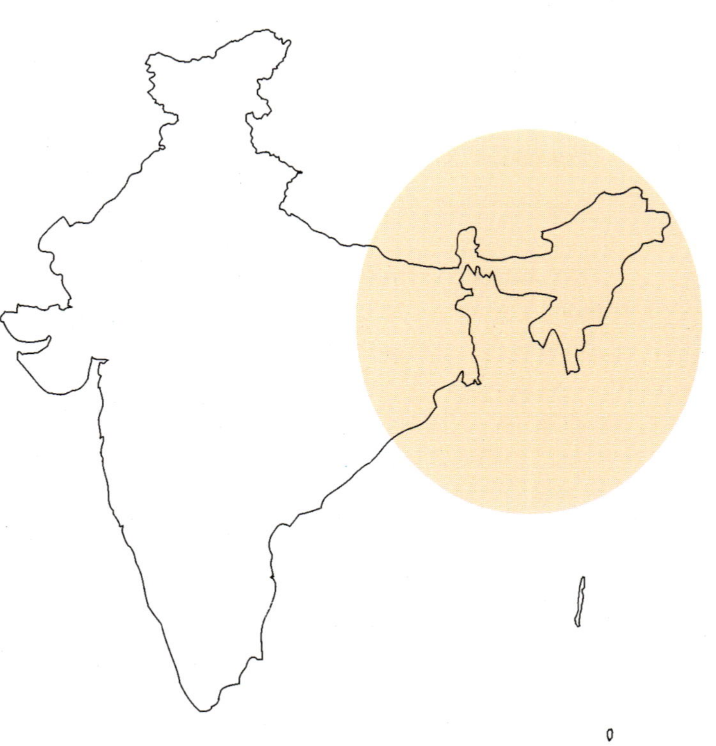

Section 2

Bhaat

1. **Bengal :** Pressure cooked *Biryani, Posto Bhaat,* Non-vegetarian *Khichuri, Fish Kofta Pulao, Pulao with Parwal* and *Pulao with Raw Jackfruit (Kathal).*
2. **Orissa :** *Chicken Pudina Pulao* and strictly *Pure Vegetarian Khichuri.*
3. **Assam :** *Savoury Sticky Rice.*

The Eastern India is called the rice bowl of India. A great deal of the country's rice is grown here. Similar to the south of India, apart from rice being a staple diet, it finds itself in many food items in these parts. Ground and made into a batter for pancakes; boiled and shallow fried to make *muri* or puffed rice, it is consumed in every possible way, with slight regional variation. This is true of the three major states – Bengal, Orissa and Assam. Bihar, technically a part of the East, subsists more on *sattu* or roasted Bengal gram flour *(besan)* which provides one with strength and high energy.

Rice in the east, is eaten in totally contrasting ways. It is partaken as *Garam Bhaat,* the hot steaming rice, with *dal* or fish curry or the very cooling *Panta Bhaat,* which is actually left over cooked rice, soaked overnight in water so that it does not spoil. This is eaten with plain salt or with vegetables, and sometimes, with some lemon leaves, tossed into it. This is known *as Boyda Bhaat* in Assamese and makes a great breakfast for the people of this state.

1. Bengal

If you follow the flow of the River Ganga, Bengal, forms its last stop, as this majestic river with its origin in the mighty Himalayas, empties itself into the Bay of Bengal.

As the train hurtles into the plains of Bengal, the earth, baked red by the northern sun, gradually gives way to a verdant green of the paddy fields, dotted with ponds. Rice is the major crop in this region and an entire cottage industry exists around it. The farmers grow rice both as a cash crop and for their own consumption. Much of the processing of rice – husking, threshing, boiling, etc. take place in their backyard, as women, too, chip in with the paddy to rice relating chores, even though machines are used today.

Rice has inspired poetry, literature and children's rhymes. Those who have migrated from the once, East Bengal, later to East Pakistan and now, Bangladesh, have very fond memories of a totally agrarian society, compared with the more industrialized Calcutta, – the first capital of British India, presently known as Kolkata.

Celebrations during *Nabanna* or the rice crop harvest during January, (corresponding to *Pongal* in Tamil Nadu and *Bihu* in Assam) witnesses a symbolic rice preparation that raises a toast to the 'new rice' as the name suggests.

In Chittagong, a *Nabanna* is a drink, prepared with fistfuls of 'new rice', mixed with green coconut juice. This, in turn, is flavoured with peeled oranges!

There are a number of rice dishes that Bengal can lay claim to. Being not quite the south or the north, its cuisine mixes many strains and influences resulting in something uniquely, Bengali. Unfortunately, many food writers, fed on a staple of five-star dishes, promote only *Punjabi or Dakshinee* flavours, as the only tastes of India. Luckily, with frontiers and minds opening up, this attitude is now changing.

Bengalis who may have indulged in rich food for days, thanks to a wedding or other festivities, occasionally cleanse their palate with a meal of *Sheddho Bhat,* which is nothing but parboiled rice, boiled again with vegetables and even plain *dal.* The vegetables can range from potatoes to gourd (even bitter gourd!) to bhindi, which when boiled, becomes quite slithery! All this is cooked very fast, because most of the vegetables and *dal* are put into small but separate muslin *potli,* and are boiled with the rice! And if you thought this was bland, think again. For the mish mash is spiked with *kashundi* or a mustard sauce.

The best dishes anywhere in the world are undoubtedly cooked at home. We bring you homemade rice dishes from Kolkata, as results of tradition blending with modern innovations.

1. SHYAMALI MAMI's *Fish Kofta Pulao*

Mrs Shyamali Basu, an aunt-in-law, is an excellent cook. She could well patent some of her recipes. Her *pulao* with local vegetables like *echor,* (raw jackfruit) and even *potol* or wax gourd makes you think of so many other possibilities.

Shyamali Mami's tip for any special rice preparation is, "Cooking a *pulao* in a stock, makes it all the more tasty. *Vegetable pulao* should be cooked in a vegetable stock or even in a meat stock if you are not a strict vegetarian; a meat or fish stock can be used for *Fish pulao* but only a meat stock for a *Meat pulao,* gives that extra flavour and softness to the rice. If coconut milk extract is used, it is better to add this towards the end of the cooking."

Serves 6.

To make *Fish Kofta.*

Ingredients

500 gms boiled meat or fish (preferably boneless);

Please note: A fish like *Rohu*, *Bhetki* or *Arr* is best. The fishy smell can be reduced by marinating it either in vinegar/lime juice or even a little milk. You can also use ready-to-fry fish *koftas*/balls available in supermarkets.

• Garlic paste	½ tsp
• Ginger paste	½ tsp
• Grated onion	1 tsp
• Gram flour for binding	1 tbsp
• Green chillies	A few
• Coriander or parsley leaves	A sprig
• Oil	2½ tbsp
• Salt	To taste

Method for the Fish Balls

In a little oil, (½ or tsp.) sauté the onion, garlic and ginger paste and mix it well with the fish alongwith the other ingredients. You can add boiled and mashed potatoes to the fish. You may slightly dry roast the *besan*, which is used for binding the fish mixture.

Make a few fist-sized balls. In place of *besan*, you can add *atta* or *maida,* but there is no need to dry roast this.

In about 2 tbsps of oil, fry the fish balls and set aside on an oil absorbent paper.

For the rice.

Ingredients

• Basmati Rice	500 gms.
• *Tej Patta* (bay leaves)	A few
• *Garam masala*	5/6 small cardamoms
• Cloves	5/6
• Stick of cinnamon	1 inch
• Ghee/White oil	1 tbsp
• Salt	To taste
• Grated ginger	1 inch
• Green chillies (deseeded)	4 or 5
• Saffron	A pinch
• Sliced onions	1 big/2 medium-sized

For the stock.

Boil some chicken pieces with a little salt. You can make fish stock too, with a few pieces of fish, a few *Tej patta* and a tbsp of parsley leaves.

Method

Put ghee/oil in an open pan and when smoke comes out, brown the sliced onions and keep aside. In the same oil, add *Tej Patta*, whole *garam masala*, and when they are spluttering, add the rice and stir it around a bit. Add the stock and cook the rice till it is almost done.

Turn off the flame. Now arrange the fish balls over the rice and bring it back on the flame. This is the time to add both the grated ginger and whole, but deseed green chillies before adding them. Add the salt. Cook covered in low heat for about five minutes. Turn off the flame. Mix a few strands of saffron in milk and add to the rice mixture. Garnish with onion slices.

Serve with a *potato raita.*

2. SHYAMALI MAMI's *Potol Pulao* or (Wax gourd) *Pulao*

Serves 4-5.

Ingredients

• Long grained Basmati Rice	500 gm
• *Tej pattas* (bay leaves)	A few
• Cardamoms	5/6 (small)
• Cloves	5/6
• Cinnamon	1 inch stick
• Ghee/White oil	2 tbsp
• Salt	To taste

• Grated ginger	1 inch
• Wax gourds *(potols)*	Roughly 25
• Green chillies *(deseeded)*	A few
• Whole *jeera* (white)	1 tsp
• Raisins or *kishmish*	1 tbsp
• Cashewnuts	1 tbsp
• Coconut milk	From one small coconut or half of one big one
• Coconut julienne	2 tbsps
• Sugar (optional)	1 tbsp

Method

(To get the coconut milk, first grate the coconut or run the coarsely chopped coconut in a mixie. Boil water in a *degchi* and add the coconut pieces till you get the adequate milk. Strain)

Please note: ready coconut milk is also available in tetra packs in supermarkets or general stores.

In about 2 tbsps of white oil, fry the wax gourds (potols) well after skinning and salting them. You may smear these with a pinch of *haldi* in which case, when cooked with rice, it will take on a yellowish tint. If you wish to keep it white, there is no need to coat the gourds with turmeric or *haldi.* Fry well but do not make it too crisp. Keep aside on an oil absorbent paper.

In about 1 tsp of little ghee, fry the sliced coconut and keep aside.

In a pan, add the ghee/white oil, *tej patta, garam masala, jeera* and when spluttering, add the rice and stir it around for sometime with all the other ingredients in the pan. Add adequate water and cook till its almost done. The Basmati Rice cooks quickly, so keep a close watch that the grains remain loose, yet soft and do not get overcooked.

Switch off the flame. Now arrange the wax gourd over the rice. Add the coconut milk, grated ginger green chillies, raisins and cashewnuts and mix it up a bit. Cook for a few minutes more. Add the salt. Scatter the fried coconut and keep it covered on the gas by putting off the flame for sometime, before serving it hot.

Please note: This *pulao* can also be made sweet too if cooked with coconut milk, which is often sweet. While cooking the sweet pulao you may add about one big tablespoon of sugar.

3. MAMI's *Rice with Echor*

There is another variation to this rice which can be cooked with *echor* or jackfruit, eaten as a vegetable in Bengal, before it ripens into a fruit. In Bengal, it is known as *kathal* only when it ripens. It is often made into a rich spicy curry in Bengal, the vegetarian equivalent to a mutton curry.

In this case, cube about 20 pieces of *echor*, smear with *haldi* and salt and steam, till adequately soft, but not overdone.

In a pan, add one big grated onion, half a teaspoon of garlic paste and the same amount of ginger paste and one teaspoon of chilly powder. Add the cubed *echor* pieces and fry around for sometime till the spices are absorbed into the vegetable. Keep aside.

In a pan, add either ghee or white oil.

Please note: For pure vegetarian dishes, ghee is always a better option than oil in matters of taste. Now, add the same amount of *garam masala* and whole *jeera*, as mentioned in the previous recipe for the same amount of rice, i.e., 500 grams of Basmati.

After stirring it around for sometime, add water and cook till almost done. Now mix the *echor* with the rice, add one inch of grated ginger and three to four deseeded green chillies. Cook for sometime more in low heat. There is no need to add coconut milk. Garnish with raisins and cashewnuts.

More Rice Preparations from Bengal

The following three recipes are from my mother, Mrs Archana Majumdar's kitchen. Her trademark is sheer simplicity, combining her own West Bengali (*Ghoti*) culinary style, (this explains the inclusion of rice with posto or khus khus) with *Bangal* (East Bengal) strains from my father's side.

4. MA's *Pressure cooked Biryani*

I still remember the day my mother cooked her first Biryani. She wanted to also try the new pressure cooker. But the results were a bit disastrous, as the rice went a bit soggy so it was christened *Bir-Khichdi* (a mix of *Biryani* and *Khichdi*) by her critical children.

This made her more determined as ever and since practice makes one perfect, both her *pulao* and *biryani* today emerge just right as she says, "Get the water amount right and you can never go wrong!"

Now this may seem a bit of an oxymoron as *biryani* is best cooked on slow heat for a very long time, till the flavour of all the spices and meat blend with the rice. But in today's times, we are inclined towards shorter routes in cooking. The choice is yours.

The cooker does help in sealing all the aromas. So keep it inside the cooker for sometime, even after switching off the flame.

The question may also rise why are we choosing *biryani,* when we are accenting on the East which has a vast repertoire of other rice dishes? But, as mentioned before, *biryani* evolved in various ways throughout the country, remaining as it does, a very popular dish. It not only works best with succulent pieces of mutton but the secret is in the correct seasoning of both the rice and the meat, with the correct spices, which in this case, comes closest to the North Indian concoction. Yet, it is uniquely a Kolkata dish, as available in many eateries, big and small, as also by the roadside.

Serves 6-8.

Ingredients

• Mutton	1 kg
• Basmati Rice	1 kg
• Sour curd	$3/4^{th}$ of a cup
• Red chillie powder	2 tsps

• Ginger paste	2½ tsps
• Cumin powder/paste	2 tsps
• Coriander powder/paste	2 tsps
• *Shahjeera*	1 tsp
• *Shahmorich*	1 tsp
• Onion	3 (chopped into fine pieces)
• *Tej patta* (bay leaves)	3
• Garam masala	(make two separate portions)
• Small cardamoms	12
• Cloves	6
• Nutmeg	½ tsp
• Mace	2/3 strands
• Salt	To taste
• *Kewra* essence	A few drops
• Saffron strands	$1/4^{th}$ tsp
• Ghee/White oil	2/4 tbsp

Method

Heat about 2 tablespoons of ghee in a pressure cooker. Add chopped onion, garlic and ginger paste, cumin and coriander, and fry these around a bit before adding the mutton pieces. Now add the chilly powder, one portion of the *garam masala, shahjeera, shahmorich*, salt to taste and curd. Stir these around well so that the meat pieces are well covered with the spices. Let it simmer for about five minutes. Now add adequate warm water and cook for about 5 to 7 minutes, first on high heat, till the first whistle and then on medium flame. Put off the flame and let the cooker remain with the lid tight for sometime.

Decant the meat pieces and separate the stock.

Put the remaining 2 tablespoons of ghee in a *handi*, add the remaining portion of the *garam masala* and bay leaves and lastly the rice. Fry it around and then add about three cups of water and cook, till it is three-fourth done.

Make two portions of the rice. In half the portion, layer the rice with half the amount of the mutton and cook in half the stock and saffron mixed with one tablespoon of milk or one teaspoon of rose water.

Cook till the first whistle only.

In the same way, cook the other portion of the rice, meat and stock, but without the saffron.

Finally, mix the two portions, so that half the rice is pale yellow while the other half is white. Sprinkle *kewra* water only if you have not already added the rose water with the saffron. Cover and keep for sometime before serving.

If you wish to add potatoes, boil the whole medium-sized potatoes – about eight and stir fry these till they become a nice red in colour. Again divide into two portions and pressure cook with the rice and meat so that they become both tender and flavoured with the meat and spices.

When making a *Chicken Biryani,* the entire process of cooking the chicken and the rice can be done at one go, with all the ingredients put inside a pressure cooker and fried for ten minutes. Put the water accordingly to cook the whole thing.

5. MA's *Rainy Day Khichuri*

Kedigree, porridge or a gruel, you name it and it is a *khichdi*, for you. Whether cooked with only rice or with one or more lentils, *khichdi*, as the name suggests, is a pish pash but not quite so bland.

Though a *khichdi* may have originated under duress, when just the basic ingredients like rice and dal are available to the housewife, it can be made into a reasonably tasty dish.

In Bengal, the *khichuri* as it is pronounced, is always associated with a rainy day. Only *chawal*, *dal* and a few onions were all that were needed to make this dish, which today has undergone a transformation in the hands of various cooks.

The popularity of this dish *(Ma's Rainy Day khichuri)* lies perhaps in it being a one-dish meal for vegetables (tastes great with peas and cauliflower) and even left-over meat can be tossed into it and seasoned with various spices. Served with pickles, *papad*, butter and fried *bhajis* and topped with ghee or butter, sometimes one almost wishes for the rain.

Serves 5-6.

Ingredients

• Rice	1 cup
• *Masur dal*	1 cup

• Cubed mutton	250 gm (preferably cooked)
• *Tej patta* (bay leaves)	A few
• Ginger	1 tsp
• *Jeera* (whole seed)	½ tsp
• *Haldi* or turmeric powder	½ tsp
• Red chillie powder	½ tsp
• Onion	1 big (sliced)
• Green chillies	4/5
• Whole *garam masala*	1 tsp of (2 *elaichis*, 2 *laungs*, a little *dalchini*)
• Oil	½ tbsp
• Salt	To taste

Method

In a pressure cooker, add the *tej patta* or the bay leaves, sliced onions and meat pieces and fry for sometime with the other powdered spices, starting first with the whole white *jeera* and ginger paste.

Now add first the *dal*. Fry around in the mixture and then the rice and finally, the slit green chillies. If mutton is not cooked, this can be added now, cubed into small pieces.

Cook in about two-and-half cups of water. Lower the flame, after the first whistle and cook on low heat for at least 25 minutes. Before taking it off the fire, pound the whole *garam masala* and sprinkle over the cooked *khichuri*. Cover and keep for a couple of minutes.

Serve hot with mango or lime pickles or mango or tomato sweet *chutney* and *papad*.

6. GRANDMA's *Posto Bhaat*

Given more to vegetarian dishes, my grandmother who hailed from West Bengal, adored *posto or khus khus.* Here is a simple rice dish with it.

Serves 3-4.

Ingredients

• Raw rice or left-over rice	1 cup
• *Posto* or *khus khus*	1 tbsp
• *Jeera* seeds	½ tsp
• Mustard oil	1 tsp
• Green chillies	2 slit
• Salt	To taste

Method

Make a paste (*silbatta* or in a mixie) with *khus khus/ posto,* one green chillie and a pinch of mustard oil.

Add the rest of the mustard oil in a pan and when smoking, add the *jeera* and green chillies. When the crackling sound comes, add rice and fry around a bit before adding the poppy paste and cook it in a hint of water.

If cooking with raw rice, first cook the rice till it is almost done. Then mix it with the poppy seed paste or posto and cook it together with just about that much water which would fully cook the rice, without making it too soft. This kind of rice is also prepared in some parts of Bihar and is relished a lot.

2. Orissa

Oriyas are said to be one of the finest and best cooks in the country. They are adept at cooking any kind of cuisine and a casual count in leading hotels and medium eateries is bound to throw up a number of Oriya chefs.

There are major similarities between Oriya and Bengali styles of cooking. Nevertheless, every state has its own special touch lent to popular dishes. Mrs Manasi Ghosh comes from Bhuvaneshwar. Both she and her husband – a weekend cook – enjoy cooking, working out the most simplest of ways in getting a dish well done.

Mrs Ghosh's *Chicken Pulao* cooked with *pudina* or *mint leaves* and *curd*, is a lovely mélange of colours such as yellow, if you use saffron and a pale shade of green due to the mint leaves.

She also gives a recipe for a *khichuri*, a variation on the pure vegetarian one cooked in the state temples (as Orissa is known for its many temples) as *bhog* or *prasad* of the deity.

1. MANASI's *Chicken Pudina Pulao*

Serves 4-6.

Ingredients

• Basmati Rice	500 gms
• Chicken	½ kg (cut into medium-sized pieces)
• *Pudina* or mint leaves	A bunch
• Thick curd	1 cup
• Ginger paste	1 tsp
• Garlic paste	1 tsp
• Chilli powder	½ tsp
• Biryani Masala	1 tsp
• Onion	1 large (sliced)
• Salt	To taste
• Oil	2 tbsps
• Strands of saffron	A few immersed in milk. (optional)

Method

Clean, wash and boil the rice with some salt and nine to ten mint leaves, without their stems, till its three-fourth done. Keep aside.

In a pan, add oil and fry the sliced onion till golden brown. Toss in the chicken, cut into medium-sized pieces along with the spices–that is, garlic, ginger, chilli powder and *Biryani Masala*. Add the remaining mint leaves (leaving a few) and curd and let it cook for sometime, i.e., about 10 minutes.

Take a *handi* or pot and grease it well with one teaspoon of ghee. Layer the rice and chicken pieces alternately and cook in the chicken stock (by boiling a few chicken bones) after covering the pot tightly with a lid. Add saffron. Place it on a *tawa* or pan. Increase the flame to high heat for about five to seven minutes. Lower the flame and keep it on for about the same duration.

The rice will have, by this time, cooked fully and blended well with the meat and spices.

Serve hot with onion *raita,* garnished with mint leaves.

You can also prepare ***Fish Pudina Pulao*** and ***Paneer Pudina Pulao*** in a similar way, by preparing both before. Cooking time for both will be less than ***Chicken Pudina Pulao.***

2. Pure Vegetarian *Khichuri*

In Bengal, as we have seen in the previous chapter, *khichuri* is prepared with equal portion of rice and *dal.* In some cases, two kinds of *dal* may be used, for instance, *Moong* and *Masoor,* but the total portion of the *dal* used, is usually the same as the portion of rice. "In Orissa," Mrs Ghosh informs me, "There is a slight variation. The quantity of rice used is more than the dal."

Serves 4.

Ingredients

- *Gobinda Bhog* rice — 1 cup
- *Moong* or *Masoor dal* — 1/4th cup
- Sliced Onion — 1 big
- Dry red chillies — A few
- Grated ginger — 1/2 tsp
- *Haldi* or turmeric powder — 1/2 tsp
- Sugar — (optional)
- Salt — To taste

• Whole *Garam masala*	3 small *elaichi*, a couple of *dalchini* sticks and 5 *laung*
• Oil	1 tbsp

Method

Heat 1 tbsp of white oil or ghee and when smoke comes out, add the red chillies, sliced onion, grated ginger, whole *garam masala* and *haldi*. You may add a pinch of sugar. Stir in the rice and fry well. Now, add *dal*. Add water accordingly and cook for 15 minutes or at least half an hour, if in an open vessel.

Serve with fried *pakoras*.

In the temples, this *khichuri* is served to thousands of devotees as *prasad* and is made similarly, but without onions and with liberal doses of ginger and *garam masala*.

3. Assam

In Assam, as in most of the states comprising the North-East, rice is the favoured staple food. But with a difference. The consistency of this rice is very sticky. It is also referred to as the *bora chawal*, when newly harvested during Bihu.

Whether cooked as a savoury or in a sweet dish in Assam, this darkish red looking grain, gives a special flavour. I once asked Sukanya, a friend of my daughter, what she missed most, being away from home and studying at the North Campus, Delhi University. She replied, "sticky rice!" My search for it started my quest for a rice book on that day when I realized our country's culinary diversity, preferences and how little we know of it.

My prayers were soon answered when Mrs Rai Sharma, Sukanya's mum arrived in Delhi to be with her daughter and cooked this to the delight of us all.

Mrs Rai Sharma's *Savoury Sticky Rice*

Serves 3-4.

Ingredients

• Rice	300 gms (Boil in half the amount of water)
• Grounded ginger	10 gm

• *Garam Masala*	3 to 5 *elaichi* pieces, half a stick of *dalchini*;
• Red chillies	2
• Ghee	1 tbsp
• Salt	To taste

Method

In a pan, put ghee, add onion and chillies, grounded *garam masala* and the boiled rice. Stir around well for about five minutes. If you wish to add some chicken or vegetables like potatoes or cauliflower, etc., you may add this before adding the rice, and let it cook till it is done.

After adding the rice, fry the rice with all the add-ons and since it is already boiled, it will be of a nice dry texture. Spread a teaspoon of ghee and garnish with chopped coriander leaves.

South India

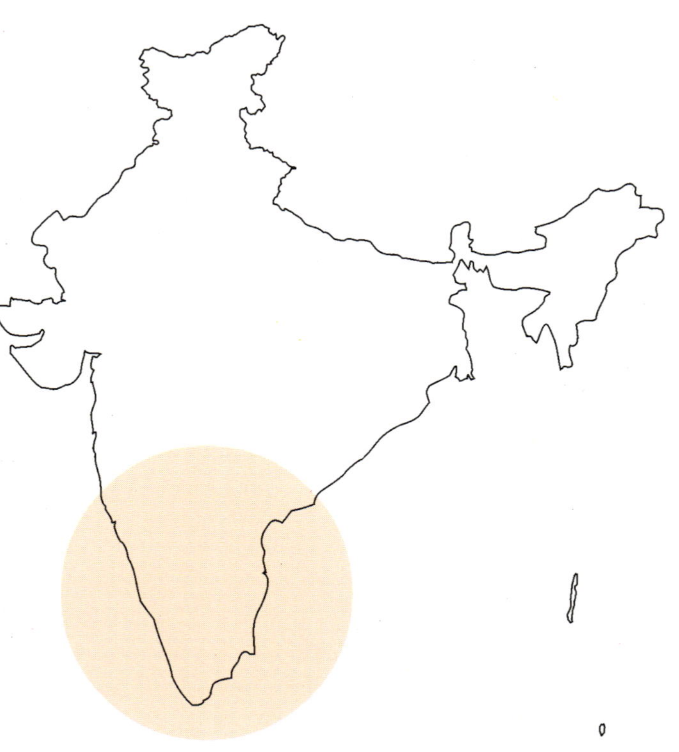

Section 3

Anna or Saadam

In the South, rice is popularly known as *Anna* or *Saadam.*

1. **Vegetarian Rice :** Venpongal, Brinjal Rice, Mint Mixed Vegetable Rice, Lemon Rice, Curd Rice and innumerable such rice varieties.
2. **Non-Vegetarian Rice :** Mutton Chettinad Biryani, Andhra Shrimp Pulao, Hyderabadi Dum Murgh Pulao, Chicken Biryani from Karnataka, Kochi Seafood Pulao, etc.

No rice book can ever be complete without a comprehensive look at the entire south of India that breathes, dreams and eats rice after cooking it in various ways. In short, South India lives on rice and we in the rest of India, are richer for some of its quick-to-prepare rice dishes.

Whether it is eaten as a staple food or as a major ingredient in snacks, rice is eaten all over the south of India, comprising the states of Andhra Pradesh, Karnataka, Tamil Nadu and Kerala.

The various *tiffin* time snacks, as rice is eaten as an early lunch in traditional South Indian homes, are also made from rice; first grounded and then fermented, alongwith *urad dal.* These snacks include *idlis, dosas, appams, uttapams,* etc., and are popular throughout the country.

In addition, there are many prepared rice dishes that are typical of the south. Some of them have received an innovative touch at the hands of an imaginative cook – for instance, rice cooked with apples!

This section refocuses on dishes that can be adapted anywhere, yet retaining a unique flavour, due to certain typically southern spices and a host of ingredients. Apart from the simple rice dishes that can be created in a jiffy, like the lemon or curd rice, often made with left-over rice, more elaborate *non-vegetarian recipes* have come from the *Malabar coast*, from Chettinad area of Tamil Nadu and Hyderabad – the royal city of the *nawabs* and *begums.*

Instead of dividing this section into chapters, corresponding to the different southern states, it is simply classified as vegetarian and non-vegetarian. From Tamil Nadu, comes the vegetarian dishes, thanks to my Tamil Brahmin friends. However there is a *Chettinad Mutton Biryani* though. Included are also two non-vegetarian rice preparations, one each from Kerala and Karnataka, though I believe a couple of the vegetarian dishes are common to the entire south. For example, what is known as *Thayir Saadam* in Tamil Nadu, is known as *Masuru Anna* in Karnataka.

Vegetarian Rice Dishes

"The most common rice dishes that are prepared in Tamil homes are *Lemon Rice, Tamarind Rice, Coconut Rice, Sambar Rice and Brinjal Rice.* This is in addition to all the main dishes, which are eaten with rice. Even *Rasam*, the soup like accompaniment is eaten with rice in the south of India," enlightens my friend and writer, Sudha G.Tilak. She continues, as she prepares one of her rice dishes for our lunch, "*Kootu* or mixed vegetable stew and all varieties of *Kuzhambu*, roughly translated into broth, is also eaten with rice." The most popular rice dishes are cooked *pulao* with a squeeze of lime, begetting a nice yellow lemony colour due to *haldi* or turmeric powder that is added to it. Similarly, rice is cooked with vegetables, coconut and with a herb like *pudina*, which gives these a distinct flavour and colour. Actually, most of these rice dishes prepared in the south are a complete dish in itself.

"Most Tamils will recollect childhood memories of travelling by train and having such prepared rice items for meals during overnight train journeys. These would be mixed at home and packed in parcels made of banana leaves and folded in newspaper sheets to keep the moisture intact and avoid leaking. It also made life easier for the lady of the travelling family to drag her food basket and dish out these food parcels to family members," says my friend Sudha, who taught me her vegetarian rice specialities.

"Prepared rice is also made at homes on special occasions and weddings. In traditional Tamil Brahmin communities, a wedding lasts for three days. The last day is called *"kattu saadam koodai day."* (It literally means, 'the day of prepared rice in packets'). Elders fondly recall the above name, because in the early days of the former century, the groom's family would set off from the wedding hall, at the bride's hometown or village to their own, often by bullock carts. As the years passed by, the journey took place in trains taking the brides further off from their ancestral village. However, the bride's family was responsible for feeding the groom's brood en route and they would make packets of mixed rice with wafers, fritters and *papads* to crunch with the rice meal along with vegetable pickles like those made with mango or lime to go with curd rice.

Rice and Pongal

Sudha is a storehouse of information as she says, "Pongal means 'overcooked rice' and it is also the name of a harvest festival in Tamil Nadu which lasts for three days. It comes in the middle of January. On this day, in rural Tamil Nadu, villagers gather in their fields for Thanksgiving to the Sun God for providing a bounty harvest. Women gather in the fields and draw elaborate *kolam*, the geometrical and floral patterns of rice flour on the ground. They gather firewood and cook the rice out in the open. A special brassware pot is decorated with turmeric leaves and marked with sandal and vermilion dots. In it, rice, milk and sugar is cooked, until the rice is overcooked into a soft consistency and the milk frothed over. This moment in earlier days was considered auspicious and is even today, usually marked by women, ululating with the farmers chorusing "Pongal-o-Pongal" and is considered an auspicious moment in the villages and interiors of Tamil Nadu.

"On the third day of Pongal, called *Maatu Pongal* (Pongal for cattle), small lemon-sized balls of rice coloured in turmeric and vermilion, and sweet white rice, not meant for human consumption, are placed on turmeric leaves and left in the open early in the mornings by the ladies of the house for a feast for the crows. On the fourth day, called *Kanum Pongal* (day of sightseeing), the ancient custom was to make the aforementioned lemon, coconut, tamarind and curd rice in packets and go on picnics. These days everyone in Tamil Nadu lands up on the beachfront or at amusement parks, restaurants and fast food joints. "Another common breakfast dish in Tamil Nadu is *Ven Pongal* (white cooked rice). This is a dish that tastes mildly bland, but is easy to digest and is filling until the lunch time," adds Sudha, providing the next three recipes.

1. *Ven Pongal*

Serves 3.

Ingredients

• Raw rice	1 cup
• Green gram *dal*	½ cup
• Mustard seeds for sauté	½ tsp
• Peppercorns	½ tsp
• Ginger	½ inch cut into juliennes
• Cashewnuts	A few
• Asafoetida powder	A pinch
• Ghee/white oil	1 tbsp
• Curry leaves	A few
• Salt	To taste

Method

Wash and clean rice and green gram *dal* and boil them together in a pressure cooker or in an open cooker with 3 and ¼th cups of water and salt to taste, so that it is really soft and gooey. Take a small sauté pan and pour the ghee or oil and when it reaches a smoking point, toss in the mustard seeds, peppercorns until they sizzle.

Switch off the flame and in the simmering ghee, add the ginger juliennes, cashewnuts and curry leaves. Toss this into the boiled and cooked rice and mix well.

This *Ven Pongal* is served with coconut *chutney* as an accompaniment.

2. *Brinjal Rice*

Please note that all the prepared rice, unlike *Ven Pongal,* are made by cooking rice and cooling it first, and then mixing it with whatever flavour – be it vegetables, lemon, coconut, etc. They are never cooked together. The rice is never overcooked. Rather it is of a *pulao* consistency, dry and loose.

Serves 4-6.

Ingredients

• Raw rice	1½ cup
• Small purple/green brinjals	6
• Onion	1 large or 2 small
• Red/green chillies	2
• *Masala* powder	Grind together 2 cloves, 1 tsp Poppy seeds, ½ tsp. *anise* seeds, 3 cloves, 3 small *elaichi* and 1 inch cinnamon stick
• Mustard seeds	1 tsp
• Bengal gram dal	1 tsp
• *Haldi* or turmeric powder	1 tsp
• Curry leaves	A pinch
• Salt	To taste
• Sesame or any refined oil	1 tbsp
• Sugar	½ tsp

Method

Clean and wash rice. Cook fully so that it is just done correct and not overcooked. Finely chop the onions. Slice the brinjals and soak them in water for 10 minutes to reduce their bitter taste. Take a round *kadai* or wok and heat it. Add a tablespoon of sesame oil. When oil is heated, toss in the mustard seeds, red/green chillies, Bengal gram *dal* and let these splutter. Toss in the curry leaves too so that they turn crisp in the oil. Add onion and fry until transparent. Add the brinjals and sauté for a few minutes. Now add turmeric powder *(haldi)*, sugar and masala powder and cook with half a cup water so that the brinjals are well done and tender. Add salt. Once the water dries and the vegetables are cooked, set them aside and cool. Then add this mixture slowly into the cooked rice and mix well. Set aside for twenty minutes before serving.

This is served with *papad* or potato chips or with a yoghurt *raita* made with beaten curd, salt and lemon juice to taste.

3. Mint Mixed Vegetable Rice

Serves 4.

Ingredients

• Rice	2 cups (cooked)
• Mint leaves	2 bunches
• Onion	2
• Peas shelled	½ cup
• *Hing* powder	¼ tsp
• Carrots	2
• Peanuts/cashewnuts	1 tsp
• Refined oil	1 tbsp
• Salt	To taste
• Mustard seeds	1 tsp
• Turmeric powder	1 tsp
• *Sambar* powder	1 tsp

Method

Wash the vegetables and the finely chopped mint leaves, onion and carrots. Heat oil in a frying pan and toss mustard seeds till it splutters. Add the *hing* powder and nuts and fry these for a few minutes. Add chopped onions and fry. Shallow fry the mint leaves, peas and carrots, Now add the turmeric powder, *sambar* powder and salt. Add a cup of water and cook the mixture until the water dries up but the vegetables that are cooked remains a bit sticky. Let it cool and then add the mixture evenly with the cooled rice. Serve with a yohgurt *raita* and *papad* or potato crisps.

More Vegetarian Rice from the South

Another of my Tamil friend, Savita, gave me the following two recipes, which are common in South Indian homes, yet tastes differently in every home (like the *Tehri*). I had these often at her place, when as young mothers, we devised ways to keep our cooking simple and nutritious, stressed as we were with our little children.

The lemon rice is a non-fussy dish, not necessarily to be made with fine grained Basmati rice. As for the curd rice, known variously all over the southern region, is a very cooling dish, especially during the hot summer months.

4. *Lemon Rice*

Serves 3.

Ingredients

• Rice	1 cup (Boiled but take care that it isn't over-cooked)
• Juice	1½ to 2 limes
• Mustard seeds	½ tsp
• *Urad dal*	1 tsp
• *Channa dal*	1-2 tsps
• Cashewnuts/peanuts	A few
• Red and green chillies	A couple
• Curry leaves	A few
• Coriander leaves	To garnish
• White oil	1 tbsp
• Salt	To taste
• *Haldi* or turmeric powder	A pinch
• Asafoetida	A pinch (optional)

Method

Cook the rice separately and spread out to cool slightly on a flat dish. Heat a little oil in a pan/*kadai*. Add mustard seeds and allow it to splutter. Add the red and green chillies and then the two types of *dals*. Stir till slightly red. Add the Curry leaves and stir for a while till they turn a bit crispy. You can fry the cashewnuts/peanuts in a little oil separately and add to this mixture. If you wish to take a shorter cut, you can fry all this together, putting them into the oil in the order mentioned.

Add a little *haldi* or turmeric powder just before taking the pan off the flame. Finally, add this mixture to the rice alongwith the lemon juice and salt and stir gently till evenly mixed. Garnish with curry leaves.

5. *Curd Rice*

Serves 3-4.

Ingredients

• Raw rice	2 cups (Leftover cooked rice can also be used)
• Curd	2 cups
• Whole black mustard seeds	1 tsp
• Ginger	½ tsp (grated)
• Green chillies/red chillies	A few
• Salt	To taste
• Curry leaves	A few
• Coriander leaves	For garnishing
• Oil	For *tadka* or tempering

Method

Pick and clean the rice thoroughly if not using the left-over rice. Soak it for about 20 minutes. In a bowl, beat the curd into a creamy consistency. Prepare the rice in a regular way, and when it is slightly overcooked, take it off the flame and mix with the curd immediately.

When cooking with the left-over rice, mix rice and curd and then add salt and the grated ginger. If the mix is too thick or if the curd is a bit too sour then a little milk may be added. You can chop the chillies into fine pieces and add to the rice mixture.

For tempering

Heat a little oil. Add the mustard seeds, red chillies and curry leaves till the mustard starts popping and the curry leaves turn crisp. Pour this over the rice mix. Garnish with Coriander leaves. Chill before serving or have it in room temperature.

For an added effect, you can add one finely chopped cucumber and one grated carrot, too.

Non-Vegetarian Rice Dishes

This section would not have been possible without the help of many people. And in this case, it has never been a question of *too many cooks spoiling the broth.* On the contrary, inputs which have come from a variety of friends and acquaintances have enriched these dishes after being tested and tried. The following three *Biryani/Pulao* recipes come from Shafiul Ishaque who runs a delightful South Indian non-vegetarian outlet (not at all a misnomer) in Kolkata, called **Tamarind**. The master's touch to these recipes have been added by Chef Kannan, who hails from the Chettinad district of Tamil Nadu, and is well versed in dishes from the entire south.

1. *Mutton Biryani Chettinad*

Serves 6.

Ingredients

Ingredient	Quantity
• Fine Basmati Rice	1 kg
• Milk	From 1 coconut
• Mutton	½ kg (very tender)
• Mixture	100 gm (coconut, *saunf* and *khus khus* with grounded poppy seeds)
• Ghee	200 ml
• Curd	100 gm
• Ginger and garlic paste	50 gm (both)
• Tomato cubes	100 gm
• Onion slices	100 gm
• Mint leaf	50 gm
• Coriander leaf	50 gm
• *Haldi* or turmeric powder	2 gm
• Chilli powder	5 gm
• *Garam masala*	10 gm
• Salt	To taste

Method

In a pressure cooker, put ghee, *garam masala*, slit green chillies, curd, ginger-garlic paste, mutton, turmeric powder *(haldi)*, tomato cubes, soaked rice, coconut milk, salt, mint and coriander leaf.

Fry around a bit. Add water in a way that its level is at least one inch above the rice. Keep on high heat till the first whistle. Lower the heat and pressure cook for about 15 minutes.

Serve with *onion raita*.

2. Andhra Style Shrimp Pulao

Serves 8.

Ingredients

• Basmati Rice	1 kg soaked for ½ hour
• Whole *Garam masala*	5 gm
• Sliced Onion	200 gm
• Slit green chillies	50 gm
• Red chilli paste	10 gm
• Curry leaves	5 gm
• Mint leaves (chopped)	1 bunch
• Coriander leaves (chopped)	1 bunch
• Ginger-garlic paste	5 gm
• White oil/Ghee	100 ml/50 ml
• *Saunf* powder	2 gm
• Cumin powder	2 gm
• Crushed garlic	5 gm
• Shrimps	300 gm
• Salt	To taste
• Tomato cubed	100 gm
• *Haldi* or turmeric powder	2 gm
• Whole *Garam masala*	4 small *elaichi* pieces, 4 *laung* pieces, 1 small stick of cinnamon
• Water	2 litres, approximately

Method

Heat a *handi* or saucepan with oil, add the whole *garam masala* and let them split. Add onions, garlic and fry them till golden brown. Then add the green chillies, ginger-garlic paste and fry till they lose their raw flavour. Now add the tomatoes, curry leaves and let it fry for a minute. One by one add the spice powders such as cumin, coriander and turmeric and cook for about five minutes. After this, add the red chilli paste, shrimps, salt and cook till the shrimps get cooked. Add water and bring it to a boiling point. Add the rice which has been soaked for half an hour and boil it till it is half boiled. Switch off the flame.

Keep it on *dum* for 10 minutes. Remove from the *dum* and add butter, coriander and mint leaves. Serve with *onion raita.*

3. *Hyderabadi Dum Murgh Pulao*

Serves 8.

Ingredients

Ingredient	Quantity
• Basmati Rice	1 kg
• Chicken drumsticks	½ kg
• Whole *Garam masala*	10 gm
• Onions	200 gm
• Slit green chillies	50 gm
• Ginger juliennes	25 gm
• Ginger-garlic paste	5 gm
• Curd	100 gm
• Rose water	10 ml
• *Kewra* water	10 ml
• Saffron	1 gm
• Milk	100 ml
• Fresh cream	50 ml
• Mewa (grated)	50 gm
• Dry rose petals	2 gm
• Coriander (chopped)	1 bunch
• Mint (chopped)	1 bunch
• Fresh sandal powder	2 gm

• Black pepper corns	5 gm
• Black currants	5 gm
• Onion browned for garnish	10 gm
• Ghee/White oil	50 gm/2 tbsp
• Salt	To taste

Method

In a *handi/degchi*, or a saucepan, heat half of the Ghee or oil. Add *garam masala* and pepper corn and when these come to a splitting stage, immediately add water for boiling. When water starts boiling, add the rice and cook till it is half boiled. Strain immediately and keep aside.

Heat the remaining portion of the oil. Add the green chillies and ginger juliennes and cook for 5 seconds.

Add onions and cook these till half fried. Add the ginger-garlic paste and fry till they are no longer raw. Add curd, rose and *kewra* water and cook with the chicken pieces till they are done three-fourth.

Now start arranging the half-boiled rice layer by layer. For one layer of rice, add a layer of *masala* consisting of saffron, milk, fresh cream, *mewa*, dry rose petals, coriander, mint and sandal powder alongwith black currants, brown onions and chicken. You have to make portions of the *masala*, meat and rice in such a way that there is enough for about three to four layers.

Keep it on *dum* for about 10 to 12 minutes.

Serve hot with mixed vegetable *raita* made with curd, cucumber, tomato, onions, green chillies and coriander leaves.

4. *Chicken Biryani* from Karnataka

I am tempted to call this dish ***Selina's Chicken Biryani***. I once visited Bangalore to stay with an old friend, Suparna Ganguly, who is a passionate animal activist. She is so involved with stray animals that she hardly finds time to cook. Luckily, she has an excellent help in Selina, who hails from Karnataka, and is an excellent cook. She prepared this wonderful *Biryani* for lunch when I reached her place, after a three-hour train journey from Chennai.

This *Biryani* remains one of the best rice dishes I have ever eaten, though the famous spicy *Bisi Bela Huli Anna*, a rice cooked in porridge style with green split peas and other green vegetables/herbs is the best known rice dish of Karnataka.

Serves 5-6.

Ingredients

• Basmati Rice	½ kg, cleaned and soaked for 5 minutes
• Water	6 cups
• Chicken	¾ kg
• Ginger-garlic paste	50 gm
• Tomatoes	2 big ones (cut into long pieces)
• Curd	1 small cup
• Green chillies	3 (cut long)
• Red chilli powder	1 tsp
• *Haldi* or turmeric powder	¼ tsp
• Onions	2 big, (cut into long slices)
• Cinnamon	4 sticks
• Cloves	5

• Cardamoms	3
• Lime	1 small
• Coriander leaves	1 small bunch
• Mint leaves	1 small bunch
• Ghee	2 tbsps
• Salt	To taste

Method

In a pressure cooker, put ghee, *garam masala*, slit green chillies, curd, ginger-garlic paste, chicken, turmeric powder *(haldi)* tomato cubes, soaked rice, coconut milk, salt, mint, coriander leaves.

Fry around a bit. Add water in a way that its level is at least one inch above the rice. Keep on high heat till the first whistle. Lower the heat of the pressure and cook for about 15 minutes.

Serve with onion *raita*.

5. Kochi *Seafood Pulao*

In Calcutta, i.e., today's Kolkata, every Thursday afternoon, we a bunch of college students, attended a certain *Herald* meeting.

The Herald is a local Christian paper, published by the Catholic Church. In the early eighties, it was edited by the late Father, Horace Rozario, a very jovial and erudite man, who taught us the rudiments of journalism. Here, I met Shevlin Sebastian from Kerala in these meetings. Most of the *Herald* members are now spread all over India. Though now based in Kochi, working for a well-known magazine, Shevlin readily obliged with a recipe of a *Seafood Pulao*, procured from his wife, Sini.

I have christened this dish, *Kochi Seafood Pulao*, and it comes closest to *Konju Pulao*, as prepared by the Muslim *mopla* (fishermen) community of Kerala, who cook it with either prawns or shrimps.

Try it. It is simply divine!

Serves 6-7.

Ingredients

• Small prawn or crab pieces	1 kg
• Basmati Rice	1 kg
• While oil/Ghee	2 tbsps/200 gm
• Pepper	½ tsp
• Onion cut into strips	½ kg
• Garlic (grounded)	1 tbsp
• Dry chillies (grounded)	¾ tsp
• Dry Coriander leaves	2 tbsps
• *Haldi* or turmeric powder	½ tsp
• Ginger (grounded)	1 tsp

• Coconut (grounded)	2 tbsps
• Cashewnut (grounded)	2 tbsps
• Khus khus (grounded)	2 tbsps
• Curd	1 cup
• Lime juice	1 lime
• Salt	To taste

In case, you are using medium-size or large prawns, remove the shells. With small shrimps, you need to clean these in slight warm water. The crab meat can be scooped out from their shells after boiling and thus softening the pieces up a bit, when you use the crab pieces.

Method

Clean and soak rice for half an hour while you get the rest of the ingredients ready.

Heat ghee/white oil in a wok and fry the sliced onions till they turn a little brown. One by one, add the garlic, ginger and chilli pastes, pepper, cashewnuts, *khus khus* and coconut pastes. Add *dhania* and *haldi* powder. Toss in the shrimps and crab meat and stir fry. Add curd and cook it till most of the spices are absorbed.

In a separate *handi*, cook the rice in boiling water till it is three-fourth done. Drain the water off completely.

Now take a pan. Mix the prawn or crab mixture into the rice and slow cook for about seven to ten minutes in adequate water or stock, (not too much or the rice will turn soggy) till both the rice and shrimps or crabs are just done correct. Keep it covered for sometime.

Serve with a pickle, the hotter, the better.

West India

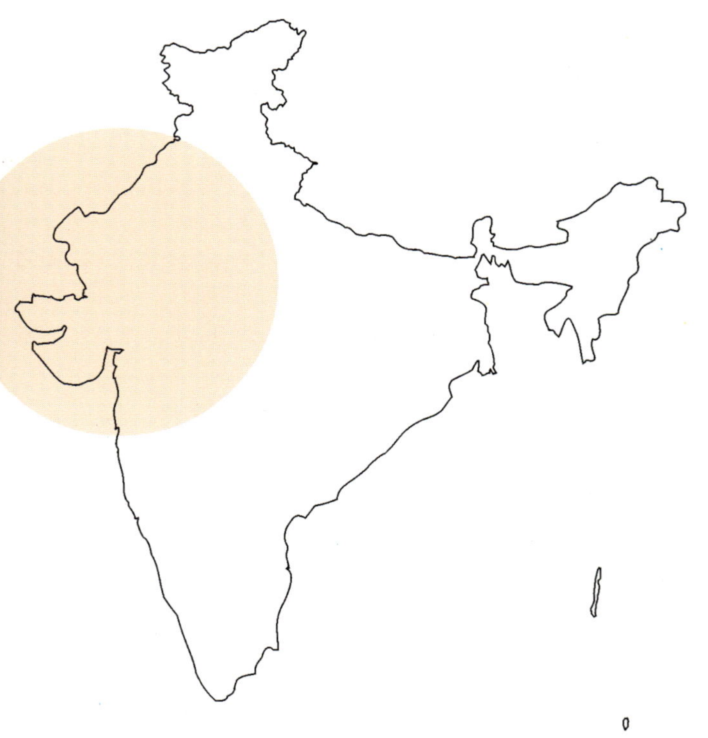

Section 4

Choka

In the western parts of India, rice is also called as *Choka*.

1. **Gujarat :** Biranj and *Dried Fruits Pulao.*
2. **Maharashtra :** *Tomato Spinach Rice, Vangi Bhaat* and *Prawn Khichdi.*

We come to our final stop, the western region, in our Indian Rice Journey. If we consider the north as more of a wheat eating zone, and both east and south as rice eating ones, the west is truly a fifty-fifty zone, because both rice and *chapati* are consumed here in equal measures.

But remember, we are not talking only about the staple food. We are accenting on special rice dishes which the western parts of India have in quite a number. Apart from the **rice cookies** called ***Anarsa*** and **steamed rice flour delicacies** like the ***Modak,*** eating rice is popular among both the vegetarians and non-vegetarians in **Maharashtra and Gujarat**.

I am tempted to add **Goa**, as Goans eat mostly rice with their side dishes made with meat and fish. But the only special rice, I have seen my Goan friends eat in Kolkata is a simple rice made yellow with either turmeric *(haldi)* or saffron or rice cooked with seafood. I have also heard of a ***Parsi Brown Rice,*** most probably browned with fried onions. Otherwise, they eat ***pulao,*** cooked with *meat and potatoes* or maybe garnished with *ida or eggs.*

---

1. Gujarat

Gujarati cuisine can be divided into three major sections. The dominantly *vegetarian fare of the Hindu Gujaratis*, the *non-vegetarian food of Bohra Muslims*, originally of Surat and the *eggs-centric cuisine of the Parsis*, who had sailed from Persia aeons back, to land at **Navsari** and make Gujarat their adopted home. All these three cuisines are well represented in Mumbai as well.

The vegetarian fare of the *Gujaratis* is a sweet affair, literally! No wonder then, their special rice or *pulao* is sweetened in sugary syrup. "This is a special rice dish called *Biranj, eaten on the day after Diwali*, which is our new year's day," informs Bhavna Thacker, a school teacher and a friend of my family, who needless to add, is a superb cook.

"It is usually eaten with a mixed vegetable dish, prepared with dry fruits or maybe a curd *raita*," she adds.

Dry fruits feature a great deal in *Gujarati* cuisine as *Mewa Biryani* of the Bohra community is a *non-vegetarian meat pulao* – rice cooked in layers of subtly spiced chicken with liberal doses of *badam* and *pista.* We include the vegetarian version and interestingly, this is eaten with a special gram flour dish called *Karhi*,(not to be confused with curry), which is very popular dish throughout Northern India. The way the *Gujaratis* prepare it, is unique and this too, has been included.

1. BHAVNA 's *Biranj*

Serves 4-5.

Ingredients

• Basmati Rice	1 kg
• *Channa dal*	100 gms
• Sugar	300 gms
• Ghee	2/4 tbsp
• Cinnamon	1 inch stick
• Cloves	5 or 6
• Cardamoms	5 or 6
• Saffron	A pinch
• Garam masala	For flavour
• Salt	To taste

Method

Soak rice and *dal* separately for about half an hour. In a *kadai*, put ghee and the whole *garam masala*, rice and dal and fry crisply. You may add a pinch of salt, according to your taste.

Heat water in a saucepan and when warm, add it to the rice. You have to add double the quantity of water to the rice and keep stirring as the evaporation process takes place. When the rice is half done, start adding the sugar, bit by bit, till all the water is completely dried and the sugar is absorbed into the cooked rice.

This dish is of a dry consistency.

2. *Dry Fruits Pulao*

Serves 3-4.

Ingredients

Ingredient	Quantity
• Basmati Rice	1 kg
• *Tej patta* (bay leaves)	A few
• Cinnamon	1 inch stick
• Cloves	5 to 6
• Cardamoms	5 to 6
• Saffron	A pinch
• Nutmeg (*jaiphal*)	A pinch
• Ghee	2/3 tbsps
• Whole white *jeera*	1 tsp
• Dry fruits	150 gms (nuts, cashew-nuts raisins, pistachios)
• Salt	To taste
• Sugar	½ tsp

Method

Heat ghee in a wok and lightly fry the dry fruits till they turn a little pinkish in colour. Keep aside. In the same medium, add the bay leaves, all the *khara* or whole spices – whole jeera and *garam masala*, and fry these for a little while before adding the rice, along with salt and a little sugar to taste. Mix well and cook in double the amount of water till the rice is cooked just right and the grains are long and separate. Mix the saffron with some milk and spread over the rice.

Serve with *Karhi* which in this case is almost like a sauce, tempered with spices.

To make *Karhi*.

- Milk (set to curd) — ½ litre
- *Besan* — 2/3 tbsps
- *Haldi* powder — ¼th tsp
- Chillie powder — ¼th tsp

Into the curd, stir in the *besan* and boil in half a litre of water. Let it boil for sometime. Add ¼th tsp of *haldi* or turmeric powder and ¼th tsp of chilli powder. Add a small piece of *kokam*. Mix well and bring it into a nice creamy consistency. No gram flour dumplings or fried *pakoras* are used in this particular version of *Karhi*.

For tempering

In a small pan, put half a tsp of ghee and add a *Tej patta* or bay leaf, a couple of red chillies, a couple of cloves, a pinch of cinnamon powder, a few mustard seeds, ½ tsp of whole *jeera*, ½ tsp of *methi* seeds and a pinch of *hing*. When roasted, pour over the curd till it sizzles. Garnish with coriander leaves or *curry patta*.

2. Maharashtra

Urad dal is known as *varan* in this state, and Maharashtrians prefer this *dal* over many others, to eat with their rice. So much so, I have heard the term *Varan Bhaat*, which rightly or wrongly, may mean both cooked/eaten together. Otherwise, this *dal*, cooked and then tempered with a bit of *haldi* or turmeric powder, salt and *hing* is eaten with rice. Other rice preparations would include a *Masala Bhaat*, i.e., rice prepared with vegetables like cabbage and brinjals or rice prepared with *pakoras*.

Vangi Bhaat is a rice *pulao* prepared with brinjals which the Tamils also prepare. The only difference being that the *Marathis* use *copra* or dried coconut in their version. The vegetarian cuisine of Maharashtra caters to the Brahmanical tastes but the state also has a long unbroken coastline. It is but natural that fish and seafood find their way into many dishes; one such being rice and *dal* cooked with prawns *khichdi*.

Tomato Spinach Rice is a special rice made by the Jews settled in Mumbai. Surprisingly, I once ate this at a Jewish friend's house in Kolkata. It was served along with some other dishes which have now erased from my memory. This one remains strongly etched for its unique taste or maybe, because it was rice.

My friend's name was Gloria Abraham and she studied in my school. Her own school *tiffin* would feature mince preparations wrapped in spinach leaves which some of us, with more adventurous taste keenly looked forward to.

Later, I learnt more about the Jewish community and their history of remarkable achievements. Their number has since dwindled in this country.

Tomato Spinach Rice is one dish made by the Jews, spread in many parts of the world, or maybe only in India, one does not know for sure. What I know is that I procured this recipe much later and with much difficulty.

---

1. *Tomato Spinach Rice*

Serves 4.

Ingredients

• Basmati/long-grained rice	2 cups
• Spinach	250 gms
• Tomatoes	2/3 medium-sized
• Onion	1 medium-sized (sliced)
• Oil	3 tbsps
• *Haldi* or turmeric powder	¼ tsp (grounded)
• *Dhania* and *jeera* seeds	1 tsp (grounded) dry or roasted
• Salt	To taste

Method

Wash the rice and soak for half an hour.

There are two ways of doing this. You may first boil the spinach in a little water for spinach gives out water when boiled. After it is soft, squeeze out the excess water or deep fry the spinach in oil, and after draining out the excess oil, set aside with the tomatoes.

Chop both the spinach and tomatoes very finely. In a pan, heat oil and add the sliced onion and fry till they first turn pinkish and then, brown. Stir in the rice and fry around for sometime. To this, now add the chopped spinach and tomatoes. Sauté the mixture after adding the *haldi* or turmeric powder, roasted and ground jeera and coriander seeds. Add salt and toss around with the rice for about five minutes and cook in low heat for about ten minutes. Fine grained rice cooks fast but with other rice, the time required to cook the rice may be longer.

Before serving, gently and evenly mix the vegetables with the rice.

The above rice recipe can be eaten without any accompaniment.

2. MRS THACKER's *Vangi Bhaat*

Bhavna, who has been mentioned by me in the previous chapter, inherits her cooking talent from her mother, who grew up in Maharashtra.

"My mother has got her own recipe books scrawled with a whole lot of recipes," she avers. "Most of these are illegible now." She managed to retrieve one, known as *Vangi Bhaat*, or rice cooked with brinjals, often served in Maharashtrian weddings.

Serves 4-6.

Ingredients

• Basmati rice	2 cups
• Brinjal	200 gms
• *Jeera* (whole)	1 tsp
• *Dhania* (powdered)	1 tsp
• *Garam masala* (powdered)	1 tsp
• *Haldi* or Turmeric powder	½ tsp
• Grated *copra* (dried coconut)	1 tsp

• Red chillies	2
• Sugar	2 tsps
• Cashewnuts	1 tbsp
• Mustard seeds	1 tsp
• *Curry* leaves	A few
• Coriander leaves	To garnish
• Oil	2 tbsps
• Salt	To taste

Method

Chop brinjal into medium-size pieces and boil these in salted water for about five minutes. Drain the water and keep aside.

Pour about one tbsp of oil in a wok. Heat and add the mustard seeds and when these crackle, add the *curry* leaves till they are crisp at the edges. Now, put in the brinjal pieces and fry lightly. Add the rice and fry.

Now transfer the mix in a pressure cooker with four cups of water and add *haldi* (turmeric powder) and salt to taste. Cook for about 7 to 10 minutes. Then, turn off the flame.

For tempering

First dry roast the cumin and coriander powder and in about one tablespoon of oil, add this alongwith dry chillie powder and *copra.* Stir fry.

Put the rice and brinjal mixture on low heat and pour the sizzling spices tempered in oil over this. Add *garam masala,* sugar and mix well with the rice. Cook for about 2 to 3 minutes more and switch off the flame.

Garnish with coriander leaves and some freshly grated coconut.

ERY BOOKS
Paneer Bonanza
New exotic and mouth watering paneer Dishes for all occasions.
55
Paneer Bonanza
51
STARTERS/SALADS/
PIZZAS/SNACKS/
VEGETABLES/SOUPS
Nutritious Mushroom Recipes
Elizabeth Jyothi Mathew
OVER 100 FAT-FREE RECIPES
PUSTAK MAHAL
Online bookstore: www.pustakmahal.com

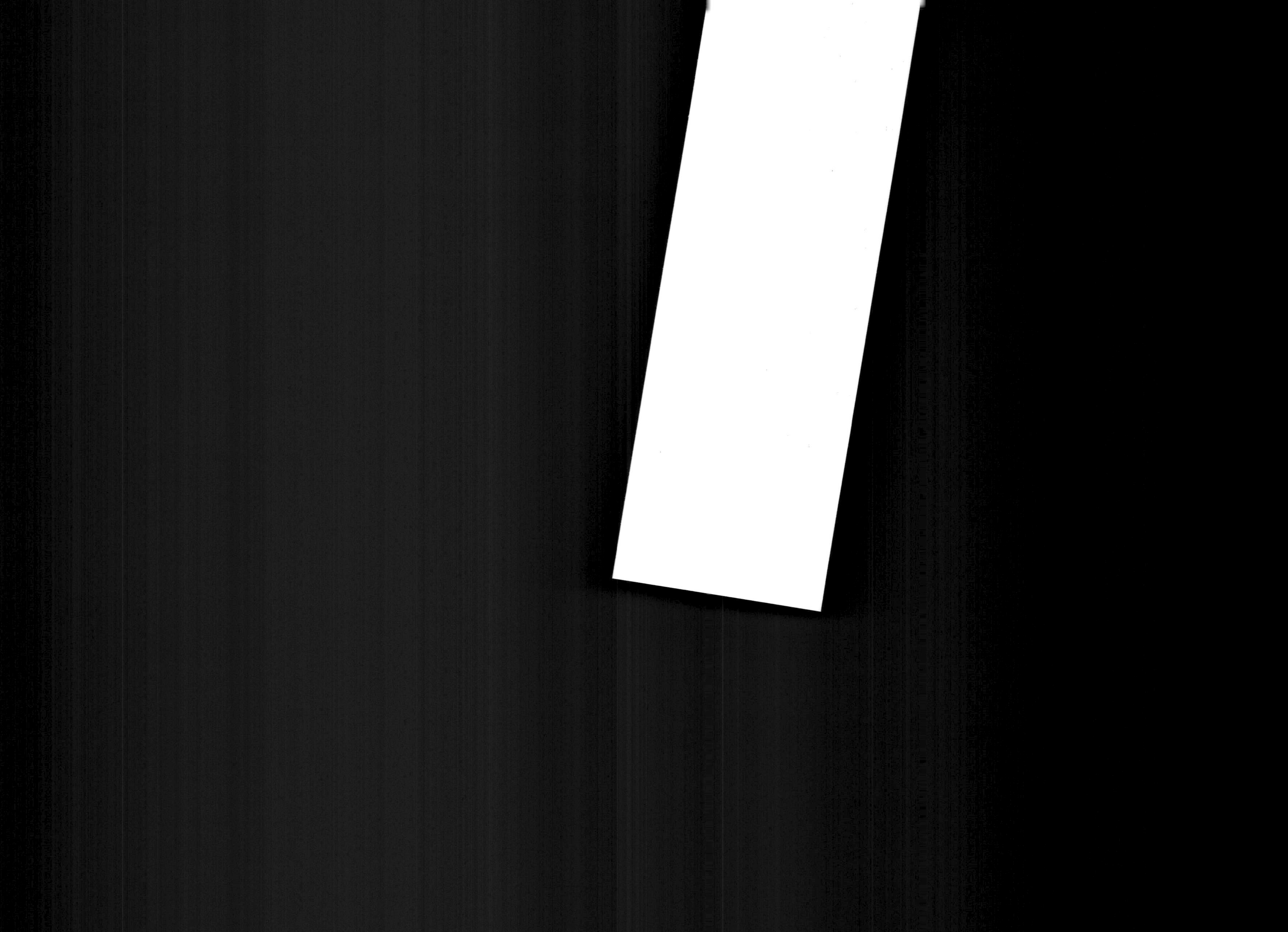

3. GEETA SETHI's *Kolambichi Khichdi*

This Maharashtrian rice recipe comes from a good friend, Geeta Sethi, who works with the UN AIDS. An excellent cook who always cooked all kinds of cuisine, when we all lived in Delhi for a while, but none of them typically *Marathi*, maybe because she was married to a *Punjabi!* She, however, emailed this unique *prawn pulao*, which she says, "Is known as Kolambichi Khichdi."

She sent me this recipe all the way from Cambodia where she was posted, a while back.

It is easy to cook. But see how rice travels!

Serves 4.

Ingredients

• Basmati Rice	2 cups (Washed, soaked for 20 minutes and then drained.)
• Garlic paste	1½ tbsp
• Ginger paste	1 tbsp
• *Dhania*	2 tbsps
• *Haldi* or turmeric powder	2 tbsps
• Red chilli powder	2 tbsps
• Prawns	2 cups (Cleaned, de-veined and washed)
• White oil	A quarter cup
• *Tej patta* (bay leaf)	1 big
• Pepper corns	12
• Cloves	4
• Small cardamoms	4
• Cinnamon	2 inch stick
• Onions	2 big (chopped)

- Coconut milk — 1 cup
- Salt — To taste

Method

Marinate the prawns in garlic-ginger paste with salt for about one to two hours.

Heat oil in a pan. Add the bay leaf and pepper corns. When they splutter, add the washed rice, salt, *haldi* or turmeric powder, chillie powder, *garam masala* and prawns. Add the salt and 3 cups of boiling water and cook.

When half cooked, add 1 cup of coconut milk. When almost done, make a hole in the centre and pour in about one to two tablespoons of pure ghee.

Cover tightly and cook till done.

Serve with chopped green coriander leaves and grated coconut.

Desserts

Section 5

Rice Dishes as Desserts

You can prepare a sweet *Pulao* and eat it with a savoury side dish, but rice is an important ingredient in preparing *Payesh* or *Payasam* or rice pudding, which explains its status in this section, strictly as a dessert.

The people of eastern and southern India, as mentioned earlier, eat lot of rice. Apart from using rice as a staple food, rice is made into a number of other dishes. No wonder then, rice stewed in milk, is a great favourite. It is equivalent to the *Kheer* or sweet thickened milk.

Long before cakes became a mainstay in birthday parties in urban India, every birthday child was given a bowl of rice pudding, prepared by either the grandmother or mother, the first thing in the morning. It was only after the child had eaten a few spoonfuls, was the rest of the family given the remaining portion. At festivities and religious ceremonies and as an offering to the gods, *Payesh* prepared well, is a sheer ambrosia.

In this section, we focus on five such rice desserts.

1. *Bora Chawal Payesh* from Assam
(Debjani Chaliha)

The uniqueness of this rice dessert is that it is made with the sticky, freshly harvested rice so popular all over Assam.

Ingredients

• Milk	1 litre
• Sticky rice	100 gms
• Sugar	7-8 tbsps
• *Pista badam*	To garnish

Method

Boil milk in a heavy bottom pan and thicken it to a creamy consistency. Add the rice and keep stirring on simmering heat till the rice turns nice and soft.

Lastly, add sugar till milk is considerably thickened.

Serve at room temperature garnished with *pista badam.*

2. *Chaolo Payesh* from Orissa

(Manasi Ghosh)

In Orissa, a delectable *payesh* is served to Lord Jagannath at Puri as *bhog.* This later, is distributed as *prasad* to the many devotees thronging the Jagannath temple. Actually, it is a small portion of rice stewed in white milk and ghee but the taste is out of this world.

No wonder the rice pudding is often described as *Paramanna* – The supreme rice.

If you prepare it at home with care, it becomes *prasad* for your family.

Serves 2.

Ingredients

• *Gobinda Bhog* Rice	1 fistful
• Milk	1 litre

• Raisins or *kishmish*	2 tsps
• Cashewnuts	2 tsps
• Sugar	1 large cup (but this is according to taste)
• Ground *elaichi*	½ tsp
• Ghee	1 tbsp

Method

Clean and wash rice and then fry it in 1 tbsp of ghee. Add *elaichi* powder. In a separate pan, lightly fry the cashew and raisins. Add the milk to the rice and let it boil, stirring it all the time so that it does not stick to the pan. After it starts to thicken, add sugar. Take it off the flame, when thickened considerably. Decorate with cashew and raisins.

3. *Chirer Payesh* of Bengal

(Archana Majumdar)

This is a bit of a digression. *Chire* or *Chidwa,* which is a by-product of rice also known as flattened rice, like *muri* or puffed rice, is usually eaten as a snack. It is made into *Poha,* a savoury *Pulao* by *Gujaratis* and *Maharashtrians,* just as *muri* is used as a base for *jhaal muri* and *bhel.*

In Bengal, a *Payesh* need not always have to be made by rice. We even have a cabbage or *lauki* (Wax gourd) pudding in which the vegetable is grated very fine and cooked in sweetened, creamy milk.

Similarly, *Payesh,* or kheer or sweetened milk and rice can be made with *chire* too instead of rice as the recipe shows:

Serves 2-3.

Ingredients

• Milk	1 litre (full cream)
• *Chire/Chidwa*	3 tbsps (the thicker variety)
• Sugar	2 cup
• Raisins or *kishmish*	1 tsp
• Slivers of *pista badam*	To decorate
• Ghee	1 tbsp

Method

Wash the *chire* (flattened rice) well, drain and pat dry. Fry it in about a tablespoon of ghee and keep aside.

In the meantime, in a thick bottomed saucepan, simmer the milk till it becomes thickened and almost half a litre. The colour should turn a little pinkish too.

Add the *chire* to the thickened milk and keep stirring till it is well blended. Add sugar and stir this before taking it off the flame.

Cool and garnish with raisins, *pista badam,* etc.

4. *Akara/Akkura Vadisal* of Tamil Nadu

(Sudha G. Tilak)

This sweet dish is special to the Tamil *Vaishnavite* community called the *Iyengars*.

Serves 3.

Ingredients

• Raw rice	1 cup (any quality)
• Green gram *dal*	½ cup
• Full cream milk	4 cups
• Jaggery (broken)	2 cups
• *Elaichi* powder	1 tsp
• Ghee	1 tbsp
• Powdered *karpur*	less than a pinch (optional)
• Saffron	Optional
• Cashew	A few pieces

Method

Wash well both the rice and *dal* and pressure cook together in milk.

Boil the jaggery in water in a separate pan. Once the jaggery has melted, it should not thicken. Now, strain and let it cool. The straining is for getting rid of any impurity that may be found in it.

In a round bottomed pan, let the rice, dal, and milk mixture boil with the diluted jaggery. When it mixes well, sauté the cashew pieces in ghee and toss it into the rice and mix well. Add a final flavour with elaichi powder and *karpur*. Decorate with saffron and serve.

5. *Rice Payasam* from Karnataka
(Brindha Nandakumar)

This is a regular *Payasam* from South India. The only difference is that it is enriched by *khoya*, i.e., thick dried milk cream.

Serves 2.

Ingredients

• Milk	1½ litres
• Water	1 cup
• Rice	1 small cup
• Sugar	2 cups
• *Khoya*	150 gms, grounded in mixer grinder
• Ghee	3-4 tsps
• Cashew nuts	5-6 pieces
• Raisins or *kishmish*	5-6
• *Elaichi*	2 pieces
• Saffron	½ a pinch

Method

Boil milk and water fully in a heavy bottomed pan. Add the rice till it is fully cooked. Add sugar. Stir it well and then add the grounded *khoya*. Mix well and switch off the flame after simmering it for 2 to 3 minutes.

Remove the container from the stove. Heat ghee. Add cashewnuts, raisins, *elaichi*, etc. to the above mixture with a pinch of saffron. Serve.

Miscellaneous Dishes

Section 6

Miscellaneous Rice Dishes

In this section, we focus on those rice dishes that have grown out of many influences and assimilations that may not seem very indigenous. This is a section comprising an eclectic mix of rice dishes, cooked with fruits, eggs, corn, cottage cheese – you name it!

The idea is to treat rice, in this section, as simply not rice but as a salad, soup, 'tiffin', snack, etc. Whichever way, enjoy having rice!

1. *Chello Kebabs Rice*
2. *Butter Mushroom Rice*
3. *Crab Pulao*
4. *Mixed fried Rice* – Indian Chinese style – Non vegetarian/Vegetarian Mixed Fried Rice – Indian and Chinese style
5. *Corn Pulao*
6. *Apple Rice*
7. *Rice in pineapple Syrup*
8. *Orange Rice*
9. *Scrambled Eggs Rice*
10. *Rice Salad*
11. *Zarda – Sweet Rice Pulao*
12. *Palak Paneer Kofta Rice*
13. *Rice Florentine*
14. *Rice in-a-Chicken*
15. *Bhuna Khichdi with Peas*
16. *Cutlet with leftover Rice*

1. *Chello Kebab Rice* (Innovation on a Persian dish)

No one can say for sure what the word, *chello* denotes, not even Kolkata's *Peter Cat*, the multi-cuisine restaurant doing some wonderful continental dishes. This is where I first tasted this dish. It is said to have originated in Persia as a single dish, that has a little bit of everything in it i.e., rice, kebabs (can be of meat or fish), vegetables, eggs and butter. It is somewhat like *skewered chicken sashlik* on a bed of rice.

The best part of *Chello Kebab Rice* is, that it is very simple. It can be easily prepared at home. Since it is served with Chicken *Reshmi* kebab and Mutton *Sheekh* kebab, you can substitute these with any kebab of your choice, like Chicken *Tikkas*, for instance, and it is equally tasty. Besides, it remains one of the best looking rice dishes ever for its harmony of colours.

Serves 4.

Ingredients

• Basmati Rice	2 small cups
• Boneless chicken	½ kg
• Eggs	4
• Small cardamom	2/3
• *Tej patta* (bay leaves)	A couple
• Garlic paste	1 tsp
• Ginger paste	1 tsp
• Chillie powder	½ tsp
• *Garam Masala* powder	½ tsp
• Salt	To taste
• Curd	½ bowl
• Capsicums	2 (big)
• Tomatoes	2
• Onions	2 (cut into rings)

Method

For at least a couple of hours, marinate the boneless cubed chicken pieces in curd with garlic and ginger paste. Prick the chicken pieces with a fork so the *masala* and the curd get into them, both flavouring and softening these. Add chilli powder, *garam masala* powder and salt. Set aside in a bowl.

Boil half a pan of water and cook the fine Basmati rice. Add a few small cardamoms and bay leaves. When done, drain the water and keep aside.

In a little oil, stir fry the capsicum, tomato and onion rings. Keep aside.

Grill the chicken pieces in an oven for about 20 minutes. Just before taking it out, cover it with the vegetable rings for about 5 minutes so that these too have a slightly crisp grilled taste.

Poach/fry four eggs separately and keep aside.

Now arrange a small bowl of rice in the centre and decorate with *Chicken* Kebabs and alternately with tomatoes, capsicum and onions. Top the rice with the poached egg and a blob of butter.

To make the dish appear more colourful, you may add yellow and red capsicum rings as well.

2. *Butter Mushroom Rice*

Mushrooms on their own do not have any taste, but cooked in butter or in olive oil, you can taste the difference. This dish has overtones of the Mediterranean region but can be adapted well into the Indian cuisine – only remember to keep the tomatoes, if not sun dried, at least crispy. It is a dish that has grown into its own with a mix of ingredients.

Serves 3-4.

Ingredients

• Long grained Basmati Rice	2 big cups (uncooked)
• Button mushrooms	2 packets (quartered)
• Capsicums	2 big (sliced into fine pieces)
• Onions	2 big (chopped roughly)
• Red tomatoes	2
• Grated ginger	$\frac{1}{4}^{th}$ tsp
• Garlic	6-7 pods (chopped into fine pieces (optional)
• Whole pepper corn	½ tsp
• Coriander leaves	1 or 2
• Butter	2 tbsps
• Olive oil	2 tbsps
• Salt	To taste
• Sugar	A pinch (optional)

Method

Wash, clean and dry the rice. In a wok, add the butter. When the butter melts, fry the onion till they turn translucent. Now, add the garlic pieces, quartered mushrooms and stir fry in high heat constantly so that they are done to perfection and yet remain crisp. As you go along, add the chopped pieces of tomatoes. Lastly, add the capsicum so that their green colour is retained.

Separately, fry the rice in a pan and cook it in little water till it is almost half done. Drain off excess water, if any.

In a wok, add the rice and the rest of the ingredients and mix well, stirring all the time so that the flavours mix. Add salt to taste and maybe, a pinch of sugar. Toss in some olives (bottled ones available) if you so wish. Mix well. Cover and cook for about five minutes. Garnish with basil or coriander leaves.

3. *Crab Pulao*

We have had a version of a Seafood *Pulao* in our South section. This one is cooked a little differently.

Serves 4.

Ingredients

• Long grained rice	500 gms (any variety)
• Crabs	6 to 8 (small sized)
• Cinnamon stick	1 inch
• Cloves	5 to 6
• Small cardamoms	2 to 3
• Dry red chillies	2 to 3
• Ghee/white oil	2 to 3 tbsps
• Onions	2 medium sized (sliced)
• Garlic paste	1 tsp
• Ginger paste	1 tsp
• Turmeric powder	½ tsp
• Cumin powder	½ tsp
• Coriander powder	½ tsp
• Whole *garam masala*	1 tsp
• Salt	To taste

Method

Wash and clean the crabs in their shells. Boil these in bubbling hot water. Pick with tongs and keep aside.

Heat half of the ghee in a wok and fry the onion slices till they turn golden brown.

Add red dry chillies, garlic and ginger paste and toss in the crabs. Fry. Add the spices – turmeric, cumin and coriander and fry till the time the oil and *masala* separate.

In another wok, heat the remaining ghee and add the whole *garam masala* in it. When they begin to crackle, add the rice and stir fry for sometime more.

Now add the cooked crabs along with the *masala* into the rice, preferably in a round bottomed *handi.* Layer the rice with the crabs. Add adequate water – one measurement more than the rice and seal the mouth of the *handi* well. Instead of water, you may add the crab stock. Cook on low heat for about fifteen to twenty minutes.

Decant on to a rice plate, decorate the crab pieces with wedges of lime. Garnish with coriander leaves.

4. *Mixed Fried Rice –* Indian Chinese style

Whoever has not heard of this rice dish – made the so-called Chinese way. The beauty of this dish lies in the way, the Chinese settled in India, adapted it to a pan Indian palate. For, it remains the ultimate meal-in-a-dish for not only does it use rice as its base, but in it goes a range of other ingredients namely vegetables, baby corn, mushrooms, eggs, fish and meats. All kinds of meat, liver are tossed in, shredded into small bits. But, if you wish to make yours pure vegetarian, you may just do that with any number of veggies such as peas, carrots, capsicum, cauliflower, cabbage, spring onions, etc. The list is endless. You can get hold of certain Chinese veggies like small red cabbages; a Chinese herb like *bok choy* too, but please do remember this recipe is Indian Chinese, but not smothered in sweet and sour sauce, as is often the case!

Non-Vegetarian

Serves 3.

Ingredients

- Rice — 500 gms
- Boiled and shredded chicken — 1 medium cup
- Sliced onion — 1 big

• Carrots, capsicum, peas	1 medium cup (vegetables cut into julienne)
• Boiled shrimps	Half a cup
• Mushrooms	Half a cup
• Grated ginger	2 inches
• Pods of garlic	A few
• Soya sauce	1 tbsp
• White oil	2 tbsp
• Salt	To taste

Method

Clean and wash the rice and dry it in such a way that no moisture remains. This is a very dry rice preparation (unless made into broth/gravy style) unlike a *Pulao* which is considerably softer.

Crush the garlic pods and along with the grated ginger soak in the soya sauce while you dry out the rice and get the other ingredients together.

Heat about a tablespoon of oil in a pan or a wok, and add the shredded chicken and fry these crisply. As you go along, add the quartered mushrooms and boiled shrimp so that these are stir fried as well. Take out with a slotted spoon and keep aside.

In the same oil, add the vegetables, one by one, for instance, if you are using spring onions, fry it first. However, constantly stir fry on high heat till they are done crisp. Keep aside.

In a similar way, heat another tablespoon of oil and fry the onions cut into fine slices. When they turn slightly pinkish, add the rice and stir fry. Add a little water and boil it three-fourth. Drain off the water.

Now mix well the rice with the vegetables, chicken, mushrooms and shrimps, if you are adding the last two. Pour the soya sauce over it, after squeezing out the garlic and ginger. This way, both their flavours will delicately get into the rice. Cook the rice in the chicken stock, keeping the pan covered. See that the rice gets done quickly and the vegetables remain crisp. (You can cook this in the pressure cooker till the first whistle only, so that both the rice and the other ingredients are not overdone.)

Before taking off the flame, dry out any moisture and stir fry around a bit more in a little oil. You may garnish with coriander leaves which is anyway, known as Chinese parsley.

Serve with green chilly sauce and deseeded green chillies soaked in white or red vinegar.

Vegetarian

This, too, is made in a similar fashion as the previous one, but without the chicken and shrimps.

You can cook it in stock got by boiling two ready-made soup cubes.

Since only vegetables are being used, you can toss in baby corn, bean curd or tofu.

5. *Corn Pulao*

A very quick and simple dish, origin unknown, but this recipe was provided by a student of psychology at the Delhi University. Perhaps, students devise such dishes that are easy to prepare and are imaginative

Serves 2.

Ingredients

• *Bhutta* or corn	2 to 3 (alternately a tin of sweet corn)
• Coriander leaves	A bunch

• Good long grained rice	1 cup
• Whole *garam masala*	For flavour
• Cloves	2 to 3 pieces
• Cardamoms	A few
• Salt	To taste

Method

Boil the corn in hot water and add herbs like a bunch of coriander leaves to the stock, while boiling.

Keep this aside. Save the stock.

Boil a cup of rice in this stock and add the whole *garam masala.*

Bring this to a boil.

When rice is semi-cooked, then add corn, which has been sauteed in a teaspoon of butter, pepper and salt. Mix all this and cook for a while.

6. *Apple Rice*

This rice can be made in a jiffy as a quick brunch or as a starter for *tiffin.*

Serves 2-3.

Ingredients

• Green apples	4
• Mustard seeds	1 tsp
• *Curry* leaves	A few
• *Hing* powder	1/4 tsp
• Cashew/peanuts	1 tsp
• Cooked rice	2 cups
• Refined oil	1 tbsp
• Salt	To taste

Method

Wash and grate the apples. In a wok, heat the oil and let the mustard seeds splutter in it. Add *curry* leaves, *hing* and peanuts. Keep the stove on simmer and add the grated apples and sauté lightly. Don't over cook, but sauté to keep them crisp. Add salt. Add the apple mixture to the rice and mix well and set aside for 20 minutes before serving with crisps.

7. *Pineapple Malai Rice*

This dish was prepared leisurely and lovingly in the upper class homes in Bengal. Decorated with silver and gold foil and scented with rose water, it presented the ultimate picture of luxurious dining. You can still adapt it to today's needs, especially in summer, when pineapples are in plenty.

Serves 6-7.

Ingredients

For the syrup.

• Pineapple	1 medium size
• Sugar	300 gm
• Cinnamon	4 inch stick
• Cloves	3 to 4
• Saffron	A little
• Kagji (green lemon) lime	2
• *Garam masala*	For flavour

For the Rice.

• Coconut milk	6 tbsps
• Basmati Rice	500 gms
• Ghee	2 tbsps

• *Tej patta* (bay leaves)	2
• Cinnamon Stick	4 inch stick
• Clove	10 to 12 pieces
• Small cardamoms	2
• Raisins *(kishmish)*	2 tsp
• Cashew	2 tsp
• Saffron	A pinch
• Rose water	1 tbsp

Method

Cut the pineapple into small cubes and steam. Keep aside.

Prepare a syrup with sugar in one and a half cup of water adding *garam masala*, saffron, and juice of two lemons. Add the pineapple pieces. Take it off the flame when considerably thickened. Set it to cool.

Now prepare the coconut milk, if not obtained from a carton.

Boil the gratings of one large coconut. Squeeze out the water when cooled to get about six tablespoons of milk.

In a large pot, heat ghee, the bay leaves, whole *garam masala* and when they start to crackle, add the rice. Cook for about three to four minutes. Add coconut milk. Stir around the rice. Now add the syrup – about $3/4^{th}$ cup and turn around the rice once again. Cook for about ten minutes in low heat.

Just before taking it off the fire, add raisins, cashews and a pinch of saffron. Mix well and keep covered till all the water is evaporated.

Finally, arrange the rice over an oval dish and decorate with the cut pineapple pieces. You can add some more *garam masala* (though not necessary) and sprinkle drops of rose water.

8. *Orange Rice*

Oranges were greatly used in North Bengal cooking because they were grown in plenty in these parts. When we make rice with fruits, we can make it savoury, but only when it is used with other ingredients, but when making a pulao with say oranges or pineapples as we have seen in the previous recipe, their sweetness is best retained.

For don't the Chinese too have their range of sweet and sour recipes!

Serves 3-4.

Ingredients

• Oranges	6
• Sugar	350 gms or less depending on an individual's taste
• Saffron	A few strands
• Rice	250 gms
• Ghee	1½ tbsp
• *Tej patta* (bay leaves)	2
• Clove	3 to 4
• Cinnamon	1 inch stick
• Cashew	1 tbsp
• Raisins *(kishmish)*	1 tbsp
• *Garam masala*	For flavour

Method

Peel the oranges and cleanse these of the white strands. Deseed them as well. Keep about a dozen aside to decorate.

Make an orange syrup by boiling orange peel with sugar in adequate water (approx. in 2 cups of water). When the syrup starts thickening, take the peels off and keep the syrup for a while longer. You should get at least one and a half cup of syrup like this.

Heat ghee in a pot and add the bay leaves and stir fry the rice. In a separate pot, boil water and add the whole *garam masala* for a while and keep aside as stock. Add this stock to the rice and cook till the rice is done.

In the centre of the rice, make a well and pour the orange syrup. Add saffron to one teaspoon milk and pour over the rice. Mix nuts and raisins. Keep it covered on *dum* for about ten minutes.

Decorate with the freshly peeled orange peels.

9. *Scrambled Eggs Rice*

This is what is called a very handy dish when there is nothing much at home, yet you have to feed a hungry family. Eating rice helps keep the stomach full as also cool, unlike say, bread, which is lighter.

The use of both soya sauce and vinegar lends that 'Indian Chinese' flavour to it.

Serves 7.

Ingredients

• Gobind Bhog Rice	750 gms
• Eggs	6
• Cauliflower	1 medium size
• Capsicum (green)	1 big
• Carrots	5 to 6
• Peas	250 gms
• Soya sauce	200 gms

- Vinegar — 1 tsp
- Green chillies — 3 to 4 (chopped to pieces)
- Oil — 1 big tbsp
- Salt — To taste

Method

Wash and chop all the vegetables mentioned into small pieces, but not small enough for them to break. Boil them about three-fourth, drain the water and keep aside.

Boil the rice and keep aside.

Now take the boiled vegetables and stir fry in oil, till they turn crisp. Add soya sauce and vinegar. Keep aside.

In the same pan, scramble these over a slow fire or whip up the eggs to make into omelettes; shred into small pieces. Add the vegetables and egg to the rice and mix well. Add salt. Cook for about two minutes. Serve hot.

10. *Rice Salad*

This can be served along with other dishes as a salad or it can be eaten as a light working lunch. Since this is a salad, you can add a range of ingredients to it. You can omit whatever you may not have a preference for and add whatever you like.

For example, you can make it perfectly vegetarian by not adding chicken. In place of it, you may add mushrooms. Also, you may add both along with shrimps.

In case of the latter, you boil – say half a cup of shrimps, by adding the juice of one lemon, celery sticks and dill.

Serves 2-3.

Ingredients

• Long grained rice	1 big cup
• Beans, carrots, cabbage lettuce, capsicum	A same sized cup of winter veggies, all cut into julienne
• Boiled chicken shreds	½ cup
• Chicken stock	1 cup
• To thicken the stock	1 tsp of corn flour
• Juice	One lime wedge
• Mustard, sugar and pepper	Pinches (for seasoning)
• Mayonnaise	2 tbsps
• Cream	optional
• Chopped up walnuts	A few
• Raisins *(kishmish)*	1 tbsp
• Grapes	A bunch
• Salt	To taste

Method

Boil the rice and drain off the excess water. Keep aside.

Make the mayonnaise dressing as mentioned below:

In the chicken stock, add the cornflour and let it thicken. After cooling it, add mayonnaise, cream, mustard, salt, sugar and pepper for seasoning.

Pour this dressing over the cut vegetables and shredded chicken. Add the cooked rice and mix well.

Please note: You can use French dressing in this salad if not using mayonnaise, of which, the eggless variety is available.

For the French dressing:

• White oil	1 tbsp
• Salt	To taste
• Sugar	1½ tsp
• Malt vinegar	1 tbsp

Mix all the above ingredients and shake well before pouring over the rice, chicken and vegetables. For sheer colour presentation, you may add, along with green capsicum (bell pepper), red and yellow ones, as well.

11. *Zarda Sweet Rice Pulao*

This is a sweet vegetarian *pulao*, with nice *kesri* (yellow) colour and fortified with raisins and cashew nuts. The rice should get a little overcooked so that it's a little broken, (unlike in a *biryani*) even though the best quality rice is to be used. But it should never be soggy, with the grains sticking to each other.

Serves 5-6.

Ingredients

• Basmati or Good Rice	1 kg
• Whole *Garam masala*	For flavour
• Cloves	½ tsp
• Cardamoms	½ tsp
• Cinnamons	A few small sticks
• *Tej patta* (bay leaves)	5 to 6
• Ghee	2 tbsps
• Ginger paste	2 tsp
• Red chilli paste	2 tsp
• *Kesri* colour	A pinch
• *Haldi* or turmeric powder	1 tsp.
• Ginger grated	½ tsp (optional)
• *Katori* of sugar	1 medium sized
• Raisins or *(kishmish)*	1 tbsp
• Broken cashew	1 tbsp
• Salt	To taste

Method

Wash and soak the rice for at least half and hour.

Drain away the excess water and pat dry. Mix into this the ginger and chillie paste, salt to taste and maybe, a pinch of sugar at this stage. If you wish to add a yellow colour, mix the *haldi* too but not the *kesri* colour and let it marinate for about ten minutes.

Heat ghee in a pan and add the bay leaves, whole *garam masala* after grounding them a bit. You may add the grated ginger now. When they start to sizzle and crackle, add the rice and fry it around. Add the sugar and mix well.

Add warm water – just enough in which to cook the rice, till its done soft and loose, but not soggy. After adding water, add the *kesri,* but this is optional. Garnish with cashew and raisins.

12. *Palak Paneer Kofta Pulao*

You can make this with just *paneer kofta* as well.

Serves 6.

For the *Palak Paneer* balls.

Ingredients

• Paneer (cottage cheese)	250 gms
• Sliced onion	1
• Ginger	1 quarter inch
• *Garam masala* powder	1 tsp
• Chillie powder	1 tsp
• Salt	To taste

For the *palak.*

• *Palak* (green spinach)	1 bundle
• Green chillies	A couple
• Cornflour for binding	2 tbsps
• Oil	For frying
• Salt	To taste

For the rice.

• Basmati rice	250/300 gms
• Cloves	A few
• Small cardamoms	6 to 7
• *Tej patta* (bay leaves)	A couple
• Cinnamon	1 small stick
• Salt	To taste

Method

Chop up the *palak* into tiny bits, wash, pat dry and steam slightly. Add finely small chopped green chillies after deseeding these. Make a paste by adding salt to taste.

Similarly, make a paste of *paneer* by adding the ingredients meant for the *paneer*. Brown the onions in a little oil before adding it.

Make small balls of spinach and stuff it with the *paneer*.

Deep fry and keep aside.

Make the rice as you would make a *pulao*.

Now layer the rice with the *paneer* balls and see that they do not break and keep it on *dum* for a while.

13. *Rice Florentine*

This is another dish that has turned homegrown in my kitchen though having its origin, in some western country. Connoisseurs of cuisine, will have a greater knowledge in these matters, but this one I learnt at a cookery class and have forgotten its name – was it *Chicken Florentine* or *Rice Florentine*? Anyway, it is a fusion dish of sorts.

Serves 6.

Ingredients

• Basmati Rice	500 gms
• Chicken	1 medium sized (cut into several pieces)
• Cream	1 cup
• Parsley	1 bunch
• Lemon juice	Half a lime
• Button mushrooms	Half a cup
• Sliced and browned onion	1 (for garnishing)

For chicken stock.

• Peppercorns	10
• Sliced onion	1
• *Tej patta* (bay leaves)	2
• Garlic pods	6
• Stalk of celery	1
• Butter	2 tbsps
• Salt	To taste

Method

Stew chicken pieces with the spices meant for the stock in about three cups of water. Keep aside separately both the chicken pieces and the stock.

Melt half of the butter in a pan and fry the rice (try with *Gobind Bhog* rice for it cooks faster) after it has been cleaned with a wet cloth. Add the whole stock and bring it to boil. Simmer for about five minutes till it is done.

Melt the remaining half of the butter and add quartered and boiled mushrooms after the water has been squeezed out. Add cream, a squeeze of lime, a few chicken pieces and parsley and stir fry a bit. In the same pan, brown the onions and keep aside for garnishing.

On an individual plate, arrange the chicken mushroom mixture around a small mound of rice. Decorate the rice with tomatoes, fried onions and a sprig of parsley. You can even use boiled and sliced eggs and tomato flowers sautéed in a little butter.

Alternately, put a small mound of rice in the centre, make a well and put the creamed chicken mushroom mixture inside it. Surround it with tomatoes and eggs.

14. *Rice within a Chicken/Stew* Chicken Rice

This is a whole chicken roast stuffed with a mixture of potatoes, peas, and carrots and enhanced with dry fruits. We have come across a great delicacy during Christian dinners, celebrating special occasions like Thanksgiving and Christmas eve and this chicken is often substituted by a turkey, in such occasions.

For a change, try a rice stuffing. This way you will not only get a complete dish in itself and will not have to serve the chicken with separate accompaniments like bread rolls, chapatti or rice.

(Rice within a chicken) or (Stew chicken rice) dish can be spiced up as well as made in the stew style and served to both children and adults recuperating from illness. It can make for a great meal for women, after childbirth.

Serves 4-5.

Ingredients

• Chicken	1 medium sized
• Rice	250 gms
• Milk	Half a litre
• Raisins	1 tsp.
• Nutmeg powder	A pinch
• Boiled peas	Half cup
• Sliced onion	1 big
• Flour	5 cups
• Salt	To taste

Method

Clean both the outside and the inside of the chicken well, preferably with lukewarm water.

There are two ways in which you can prepare this.

First: Heat 2 to 3 tablespoons of oil in a wok and fry the chicken after smearing it with some salt, till it is reddish in colour. Drain the oil and keep aside.

In another pan, add a tablespoon of oil, a couple of bay leaves and onions, till slightly pink. Add rice, raisins, a pinch of saffron, salt to taste and fry around a bit more before cooking for a while. Take care to see that it is not fully done.

Now stuff this rice inside the stomach of the chicken and secure it well by sewing up the open end. Cook in boiling water.

You either have the choice of retaining the gravy or dry it out after the chicken is cooked. If you keep the gravy, it will taste like a stew, which can be thickened with a teaspoon of flour. Cook for at least thirty-five to forty minutes on low flame.

Alternatively, you can first marinate the chicken in milk, (measurement given above under ingredients), with salt to taste. This should be done for at least a couple of hours after which, the half cooked rice should be stuffed inside the stomach of the chicken as instructed.

Wipe off the milk and coat the whole chicken with flour and wrap it around a foil. Place this foil in a pot of boiling water and let it boil for at least half an hour.

Both rice and chicken will get cooked this way, each drawing on the flavour of the other. Cut into portions and serve so that each portion has a chunk of chicken and rice.

Please feel free to add diced vegetables like carrots, peas and beans while cooking the rice to make this dish even more complete..

15. *Bhuna Khichdi with Peas*

Khichdi can be made in two ways. A simple pish pash or *masaladar* (spicy) and special enough to offer guests.

Serves 2-3.

Ingredients

• Rice	2 cups
• *Moong* dal	1 cup
• White cumin paste	1 tsp
• Ginger paste	1 tsp
• Red chillie paste	½ tsp
• *Halidi* or turmeric powder	1 tsp (paste or powder)
• Coconut	Half
• Cardamoms	3 to 4 small
• *Garam masala*	1 tsp (few cardamoms, ½ inch of cinnamon stick and a couple cloves paste)
• Whole cumin	½ tsp
• Fresh peas/frozen peas	½ cup
• *Tej patta* (bay leaves)	A couple
• Sugar	A pinch
• Mustard oil	2 tbsps
• Ghee	1 tsp
• Salt	To taste

Method

Dry roast the *moong dal* and keep aside.

Wash and dry the rice. Add 3/4th cardamom and keep aside. Heat mustard oil in a pan, add the bay leaves and whole cumin. When they start to splutter, add the ginger, cumin and chillie pastes and fry well for sometime. Add the rice and fry more. Add *dal*. No need to fry as *dal* has already been dry roasted. Mix well the two and add enough water to cook, taking care to see that both the rice and *dal* remain a little dry and not overcooked. Adjust water accordingly.

If you are using fresh peas, add these now. If you are using frozen peas, add these in the last.

To this add 2 tsp of coconut cut into julienne and fried in a little oil, so that they turn brownish. The rest of the coconut should be finely grated and added as well. Add seasoning by the help of salt and sugar.

Keep it covered on low heat for a while, adjusting the water from time to time. This dish has a *pulao* consistency. Before taking off the flame, add the ghee and *garam masala* paste. Garnish with green chilles.

Serve with an assortment of pickles.

16. *Cutlet with leftover Rice*

We have come to the end of the book and here is something you can do with leftover rice. If you have rice with vegetables, mash up the whole mixture and you will get vegetable cutlets, with rice in it!

This is a unique snack that helps housewives stem the wastage of food.

Rice cutlets (with leftover rice)

Take a bowl of cooked or leftover rice and drain off any moisture by squeezing it out. Mash into this, tiny pieces of one chopped onion, a couple of green chillies, tiny pieces of ginger and salt to taste. You can also add tiny chopped pieces of coriander leaves. Fashion these into cutlet shapes and keep aside.

For the batter.

Mix gram flour or *besan* in water till it reaches a creamy consistency. Add a little salt and red pepper to the mixture. Now dip each cutlet into the batter and deep fry these, till a nice golden brown colour is attained.

Alternately, you can whip up an egg, dip the cutlets into this and coat them with bread crumbs before frying them golden brown.

Serve with hot and sweet sauce, mint chutney or even mustard sauce.

Bread Bonanza

—Sangeeta Gupta

Bake Fresh & Nutritious Continental Bread at Home

Are you sick and tired of eating breads from the market? Do you crave for fresh and nutritious loaf of bread taken out directly from the oven on your breakfast table? Then baking at home is a healthy idea. Whether you're apprehensively curious or an ambitious beginner, BREAD BONANZA will help you rise to the challenge of baking delicious breads that turn out every time. Continental breads can be made easily like the Indian flat breads.

BREAD BONANZA is the first of its kind in India that explains you from basics: every succinct description of the techniques with illustrations. Every lesson will clear your doubts and lead you further to master the most common types of bread: batter bread, egg bread, white bread, whole wheat bread, holiday sweet bread, flat bread, and coffee cake.

With BREAD BONANZA at your side, making bread will become fun instead of daunting.

This book's contemporary approach shows you the way to make homemade breads faster and easier than ever before.

Price: Rs. 125/- • Pages: 152 (Colour)
Postage: Rs. 20/-

Paneer Bonanza

—Prabhjot Mundhir

New exotic and mouth watering paneer Dishes for all occasions.

55

STARTERS • SOUPS

VEGGIES • SALADS

PIZZAS • SNACK

DESSERTS

An invaluable treasury of traditiona, yet novel recipes of Paneer distilled over 50 years olf culinary knowledge and expertise.

- Easy to prepare.
- Teaches simple touches with everyday vegetables to make them special.
- Phenomenal range.

Delicious and nutritious too!

Price: Rs. 80/- • Pages: 168 (Colour)
Postage: Rs. 15-